I0844421

Table of Contents:

Chapter 1: Mastering the Art of Investing: Building a Foundation for Financial Success

Introduction:
Welcome to the transformative journey into the world of investing, where the power to create wealth lies within your grasp. By adopting a mindset rooted in knowledge, discipline, and strategic thinking, you can lay the groundwork for a financially prosperous future. Drawing upon the wisdom of successful investors and timeless principles, we will explore the essential steps to master the art of investing.

The Power of Financial Goals:
To embark on any successful endeavor, clarity of purpose is paramount. Begin your journey by setting clear and achievable financial goals. Envision your desired financial future and align it with your values and aspirations. This roadmap will guide your investment decisions and provide motivation along the way. Explore effective goal-setting strategies and engage in practical exercises to clarify your objectives.

Crafting a Personal Budget:
A solid financial foundation starts with understanding and managing your cash flow effectively. Dive into the art of crafting a personal budget to gain control over your finances. Track your income and expenses to uncover spending habits and identify areas for saving and investing. Discover practical budgeting techniques and

implement tools to create a sustainable budget that supports your financial goals.

The Importance of Saving:
Savings serve as the fuel for your investment journey. Recognize the significance of building an emergency fund and cultivating a habit of regular saving. Explore the power of compounding, where even small, consistent contributions can lead to substantial wealth accumulation over time. Real-life examples and actionable advice will guide you in creating a robust savings plan that supports your long-term financial goals.

Developing a Risk-Taking Mindset:
Successful investing requires embracing calculated risks. Overcome common fears and misconceptions that hinder many individuals from engaging in investment opportunities. Discover strategies for developing a healthy risk-taking mindset, empowering you to make informed decisions while managing potential pitfalls. Through practical exercises and inspiring anecdotes, embrace risk as an essential element of wealth creation.

The Role of Education and Research:
Knowledge is the cornerstone of successful investing. Emphasize the importance of continuous learning and research. Identify reliable sources of financial information and explore key investment concepts. Gain insights into conducting due diligence and equip yourself with the tools for informed decision-making. Becoming a lifelong student of the financial markets will provide you with confidence and expertise to navigate investment opportunities wisely.

By setting clear financial goals, crafting a personal budget, cultivating a savings habit, embracing risk, and prioritizing education, you have laid a strong foundation for your investment journey. Remember that knowledge, discipline, and strategic thinking will be your guiding principles as you venture further into the world of wealth creation. With these tools in hand, you are ready to explore the myriad opportunities that await you.

Chapter 2: Mastering the Art of Risk and Reward: Embracing Opportunities for Financial Growth

Section 1: The Power of Assessing Risk: A Gateway to Intelligent Investing
In the exhilarating world of investing, understanding and assessing risk is the foundation for making informed decisions that can lead to financial success. The power of risk assessment lies in its ability to provide a clear perspective on the potential pitfalls and rewards associated with different investment opportunities. By delving deeper into risk assessment, investors can navigate the tumultuous waters of the market with confidence and clarity, minimizing potential losses and maximizing potential gains. This section aims to provide a comprehensive exploration of the significance of risk assessment, delving into various types of investment risks, and equipping readers with a wide range of tools and techniques to evaluate potential losses and rewards. It's a transformative journey that empowers individuals to make calculated choices based on their risk tolerance, investment objectives, and overall financial aspirations.

Within the realm of risk assessment, it is crucial to understand the nature of investment risks and their potential impact on investment outcomes. The first step in this journey involves unraveling the intricacies of market risk. Market risk encompasses the inherent volatility and fluctuations in the market that can impact the value of investments. By understanding market risk, investors can become more aware of the potential ups and downs of their investment portfolios, allowing them to make informed decisions in the face of market uncertainty.

Another significant aspect of risk assessment is evaluating interest rate risk. Interest rates play a vital role in the economy and have a direct impact on fixed-income investments such as bonds and mortgages. Understanding interest rate risk enables investors to assess how changes in interest rates can affect the value of their investments, and adjust their strategies accordingly. By monitoring interest rate movements, investors can position themselves to take advantage of favorable interest rate environments or protect themselves from potential losses during periods of rising rates.

Credit risk is yet another critical factor to consider in risk assessment. It revolves around the creditworthiness of borrowers and the potential for default or non-payment of debts. By examining credit risk, investors can evaluate the financial health and stability of companies or individuals they may lend money to or invest in. This evaluation process involves assessing credit ratings, financial statements, and other relevant factors to gauge the likelihood of repayment. Understanding credit risk allows investors to make informed decisions about lending or investing, minimizing the potential for financial losses due to default.

Currency risk, an integral part of risk assessment in a global economy, involves understanding the potential impact of exchange rate fluctuations on investments. In an interconnected world, changes in exchange rates can significantly impact the value of international investments. By comprehending currency risk, investors can make strategic decisions regarding currency exposure, hedging techniques, or even diversification across different currencies. A thorough understanding of currency risk empowers investors to navigate the complexities of the global marketplace and seize opportunities for growth while mitigating potential losses due to currency fluctuations.

Lastly, risk assessment involves delving into the realm of geopolitical risk. Geopolitical factors such as political instability, regulatory changes, trade disputes, and natural disasters can profoundly impact the financial markets and investment outcomes. Understanding and assessing geopolitical risk allows investors to consider these external factors when making investment decisions. By staying informed about global events, geopolitical trends, and their potential impact on investments, investors can position themselves to minimize risks and capitalize on opportunities that arise within this dynamic landscape.

Equipped with a wide range of tools and techniques, investors can confidently evaluate potential losses and rewards. Risk assessment encompasses a variety of methodologies, including qualitative and quantitative analysis, financial modeling, and scenario planning. By utilizing these tools, investors can gain insights into the potential risks associated with their investment choices and estimate the potential rewards they may reap. Techniques such as standard deviation, beta, and value at risk (VaR) provide valuable metrics for measuring and managing risk. Moreover, understanding risk tolerance and aligning investment objectives with personal preferences allows investors to create a well-rounded portfolio that reflects their unique financial goals.

Section 2: Embracing the Tapestry of Investment Risks

Investment risks form a diverse and intricate tapestry that weaves through the financial markets, influencing the outcomes of various investment endeavors. Embracing this tapestry in its entirety allows investors to gain a deeper understanding of the multifaceted dynamics at play and positions them for success in the ever-changing investment landscape. In this extended section, we delve into the various types of investment risks, exploring their characteristics, potential impacts, and strategies for managing them effectively. By immersing ourselves in the tapestry of investment risks, we equip ourselves with a comprehensive knowledge and a wide array of insights necessary to make informed investment decisions that align with our financial goals.

Market Risk: Navigating the Ebb and Flow of Market Dynamics
Market risk is an ever-present force in the investment world, stemming from the inherent volatility and fluctuations that permeate financial markets. It arises from factors such as economic conditions, geopolitical events, industry trends, and investor sentiment. Understanding market risk enables investors to anticipate and assess potential market movements, adjust their investment strategies accordingly, and identify opportunities for growth amid market turbulence. By analyzing historical data, conducting fundamental and technical analysis, and staying abreast of market news and trends, investors can make informed decisions to navigate the ebb and flow of market dynamics.

Interest Rate Risk: Unveiling the Ripples of Changing Rates
Interest rate risk is intimately tied to the borrowing and lending practices of individuals, corporations, and governments. This risk arises from changes in interest rates, which can significantly impact the value of fixed-income investments such as bonds and mortgages. Navigating the ripples of changing interest rates requires a deep understanding of economic factors, central bank policies, and market expectations. By proactively managing their exposure to interest rate risk, investors can employ strategies such as duration matching, yield curve positioning, and diversification across different maturities to mitigate the potential negative impact of interest rate fluctuations on their investment portfolios.

Credit Risk: Assessing the Financial Stability of Borrowers
Credit risk revolves around the creditworthiness of borrowers and the potential for default or non-payment of debts. Whether investing in corporate bonds, lending money, or extending credit, understanding credit risk is crucial. It involves analyzing credit ratings, financial statements, cash flow projections, and other relevant factors to evaluate the likelihood of repayment. By conducting thorough credit risk assessments, investors can make

informed decisions, diversify their credit exposures, and take appropriate measures to protect their investments. Additionally, staying updated on industry trends, monitoring credit rating agencies' reports, and analyzing debt-to-equity ratios can provide valuable insights into the financial stability of borrowers.

Liquidity Risk: Navigating the Waters of Market Accessibility
Liquidity risk refers to the ease with which an investment can be bought or sold in the market without causing a significant impact on its price. Investments with low liquidity may pose challenges when it comes to executing trades, potentially resulting in higher transaction costs or difficulties in exiting positions. Understanding liquidity risk is vital for investors seeking to maintain flexibility and take advantage of investment opportunities. By analyzing trading volumes, bid-ask spreads, and market depth, investors can make more informed decisions, ensure the accessibility of their investments, and mitigate potential liquidity-related hurdles.

Operational Risk: Safeguarding Against Internal Weaknesses
Operational risk encompasses the potential losses arising from inadequate or failed internal processes, systems, or human errors within an organization. It includes risks associated with technology failures, fraud, compliance issues, and management shortcomings. Investors should be aware of the operational risks associated with their investments, particularly when investing in specific companies or industries. Conducting due diligence on a company's internal controls, governance practices, and risk management frameworks is essential. By safeguarding against operational weaknesses, investors can protect their investments and avoid potential losses due to internal failures.

Political and Regulatory Risk: Navigating the Impact of Governance and Policy Changes
Political and regulatory risk refers to the potential impact of changes in government policies, regulations, or political stability on investments. These risks can significantly affect the performance of certain industries or specific companies operating in regions subject

to political volatility or regulatory shifts. Investors should stay informed about political developments, legislative changes, and potential geopolitical tensions that could impact their investments. By diversifying geographically, staying updated on political news, and assessing the potential risks associated with specific regulatory frameworks, investors can navigate the ever-evolving political landscape and make informed decisions.

Reputational Risk: Preserving Trust and Public Perception
Reputational risk involves the potential damage to a company's or individual's reputation, resulting from negative public perception, unethical practices, or controversial actions. Reputational risks can have profound impacts on the financial performance and long-term viability of investments. Investors should consider the reputational risks associated with companies and individuals they invest in, evaluating factors such as corporate governance, social responsibility initiatives, and public sentiment. By conducting thorough research and due diligence, investors can align their investments with organizations that prioritize ethical practices and maintain a positive reputation, minimizing the potential for reputational risks to negatively impact their portfolios.

Section 3: Mastering the Art of Wealth Accumulation

Wealth accumulation is a pursuit that requires a strategic approach, disciplined habits, and a clear understanding of financial principles. In this section, we delve into the strategies and techniques for building and growing wealth over time. By mastering the art of wealth accumulation, readers can lay a solid foundation for their financial future and work towards achieving their long-term goals. From savings and investment strategies to debt management and the power of compounding, this section explores the essential components of building and maintaining wealth.

The Power of Saving: Cultivating a Strong Financial Foundation
Saving is the bedrock of wealth accumulation. It involves setting aside a portion of income for future use, building a financial safety

net, and creating opportunities for future investments. This section explores various strategies for effective saving, including creating a budget, setting financial goals, automating savings, and cultivating a frugal mindset. By developing healthy saving habits, readers can establish a strong financial foundation and create a surplus of funds to allocate towards investments and wealth-building endeavors.

Investment Strategies: Growing Wealth Through Intelligent Allocation
Investing is a critical component of wealth accumulation, as it provides opportunities for growth and compounding over time. This section explores different investment strategies, including diversification, asset allocation, and long-term investment approaches. By understanding the principles of risk and return, conducting thorough research, and aligning investments with personal financial goals, readers can make informed investment decisions and grow their wealth steadily over time.

Debt Management: Minimizing the Shackles of Financial Obligations
Debt can hinder wealth accumulation if not managed effectively. This section delves into strategies for debt management, including prioritizing debt repayment, negotiating lower interest rates, and consolidating high-interest debts. By implementing sound debt management practices, readers can reduce the burden of financial obligations, improve their creditworthiness, and free up resources to allocate towards investments and wealth-building activities.

The Power of Compounding: Harnessing Time as an Ally
Compounding is a powerful force in wealth accumulation. This section explains the concept of compounding and its potential to exponentially grow investments over time. By reinvesting earnings and allowing investments to grow uninterrupted, readers can take advantage of the compounding effect and accelerate wealth accumulation. This section also highlights the importance of starting early and consistently contributing to investment accounts to maximize the benefits of compounding.

Tax Efficiency: Maximizing Returns and Minimizing Liabilities
Tax efficiency is a crucial aspect of wealth accumulation. This section explores strategies for optimizing tax outcomes, including utilizing tax-advantaged accounts, employing tax-loss harvesting techniques, and understanding the tax implications of different investment vehicles. By minimizing tax liabilities and maximizing after-tax returns, readers can retain a larger portion of their investment gains and accelerate wealth accumulation.

Building Multiple Streams of Income: Diversifying Financial Sources
Building multiple streams of income is a key strategy for wealth accumulation. This section explores various avenues for generating additional income, including side businesses, rental properties, dividend-paying investments, and passive income streams. By diversifying sources of income, readers can create a resilient financial foundation and enhance their wealth-building potential.

Section 4: Unleashing Entrepreneurial Spirit: Exploring Business Ideas and Ventures

Entrepreneurship is a realm of boundless opportunities, where innovative ideas, perseverance, and strategic thinking can transform visions into reality. In this section, we dive into the world of entrepreneurship, exploring various business ideas and ventures that readers can consider as they embark on their entrepreneurial journeys. From ideation and market analysis to business planning and execution, this section equips aspiring entrepreneurs with the knowledge and insights needed to navigate the intricacies of starting and managing their own businesses.

Ideation and Opportunity Assessment: Uncovering Business Concepts
The journey of entrepreneurship begins with generating ideas and identifying opportunities. This section delves into techniques for brainstorming and ideation, helping readers unlock their creative potential and uncover viable business concepts. We also explore methods for assessing market demand, conducting feasibility

studies, and evaluating the potential profitability of business ideas. By honing their ideation skills and conducting thorough opportunity assessments, readers can identify promising business ventures and set a solid foundation for their entrepreneurial endeavors.

Market Research and Analysis: Understanding Customer Needs and Competition
Successful businesses are built on a deep understanding of customer needs and a thorough analysis of the competitive landscape. This section delves into market research techniques, including surveys, interviews, and data analysis, to gain insights into target markets and customer preferences. We also explore competitor analysis methods, enabling entrepreneurs to identify strengths, weaknesses, and opportunities in the market. By conducting comprehensive market research and analysis, readers can develop strategies to differentiate their businesses, meet customer demands, and gain a competitive edge.

Business Planning and Strategy: Charting the Path to Success
A well-crafted business plan serves as a roadmap for entrepreneurial success. This section guides readers through the process of developing a comprehensive business plan, including defining business goals, outlining strategies, conducting financial projections, and creating marketing plans. We also explore the importance of contingency planning and adaptability in the face of changing market conditions. By crafting robust business plans and strategies, readers can effectively communicate their vision, make informed decisions, and navigate the challenges of entrepreneurship.

Financing and Funding: Exploring Capital Acquisition Options
Access to capital is vital for starting and growing a business. This section explores various financing and funding options available to entrepreneurs, including bootstrapping, loans, venture capital, crowdfunding, and government grants. We discuss the pros and cons of each funding avenue, provide tips for securing investment, and highlight the importance of financial management in

entrepreneurial ventures. By understanding the financing landscape and strategically leveraging available resources, readers can secure the necessary capital to fuel their business growth.

Operations and Resource Management: Streamlining Efficiency and Productivity

Effective operations and resource management are essential for sustainable business growth. This section delves into strategies for optimizing operational processes, managing resources efficiently, and fostering a productive organizational culture. We explore techniques for supply chain management, inventory control, technology adoption, and talent acquisition. By streamlining operations and maximizing resource utilization, entrepreneurs can enhance efficiency, reduce costs, and create a solid foundation for long-term success.

Marketing and Customer Acquisition: Building a Strong Brand Presence

Marketing plays a pivotal role in attracting customers and establishing a strong brand presence. This section explores various marketing strategies, including digital marketing, social media, content marketing, and customer relationship management. We delve into the importance of building a compelling brand story, conducting effective marketing campaigns, and cultivating customer loyalty. By developing robust marketing strategies and implementing targeted customer acquisition tactics, entrepreneurs can create brand awareness, generate leads, and foster customer engagement.

Section 5: The Art of Financial Management: Nurturing Wealth and Securing Future Prosperity

Effective financial management is essential for individuals and businesses alike to nurture wealth, achieve financial goals, and ensure long-term prosperity. In this section, we delve into the principles and strategies of financial management, empowering readers to take control of their finances, make informed decisions, and build a solid financial foundation for the future. From budgeting and saving to risk management and retirement planning, this section provides a comprehensive guide to mastering the art of financial management.

Budgeting and Cash Flow Management: Building a Strong Financial Framework
Budgeting lies at the heart of financial management. This section explores techniques for creating and maintaining a budget, tracking expenses, and managing cash flow effectively. We delve into the importance of setting financial goals, prioritizing spending, and making conscious choices to align income and expenses. By developing a solid budgeting framework, readers can gain control over their finances, optimize cash flow, and make informed financial decisions.

Saving and Emergency Funds: Cultivating Financial Security
Saving is a cornerstone of financial management, providing a safety net and a means to achieve future financial goals. This section delves into strategies for effective saving, including setting saving targets, automating savings, and leveraging various saving vehicles such as savings accounts and investment instruments. We also emphasize the importance of establishing emergency funds to handle unexpected expenses and financial setbacks. By cultivating a habit of regular saving and building emergency funds, readers can achieve financial security and peace of mind.

Debt Management and Credit: Balancing Financial Obligations
Debt management is a critical aspect of financial well-being. This section explores techniques for managing and reducing debt, including prioritizing debt repayment, negotiating favorable terms, and consolidating high-interest debts. We also discuss the importance of maintaining a good credit score and utilizing credit responsibly. By effectively managing debt and maintaining healthy credit, readers can minimize financial stress, improve their financial position, and unlock opportunities for wealth accumulation.

Investment Strategies: Growing Wealth through Strategic Allocation
Investing is a powerful tool for long-term wealth creation. This section delves into different investment strategies, including diversification, asset allocation, and risk management. We explore various investment vehicles, such as stocks, bonds, mutual funds, real estate, and retirement accounts, and provide insights into the potential risks and returns associated with each. By understanding investment principles, conducting research, and seeking professional advice when needed, readers can develop a strategic investment plan that aligns with their financial goals and risk tolerance.

Retirement Planning: Securing Future Financial Independence
Planning for retirement is crucial to ensure financial independence in later years. This section examines the key elements of retirement planning, including estimating retirement needs, setting retirement goals, and exploring retirement savings options. We discuss retirement accounts, such as 401(k)s and IRAs, as well as the importance of taking advantage of employer-sponsored retirement plans and maximizing contributions. By starting early and consistently saving for retirement, readers can build a nest egg that supports their desired lifestyle during the post-working years.

Risk Management and Insurance: Safeguarding Financial Assets
Risk management is an integral part of financial management. This section explores the role of insurance in protecting financial assets and mitigating potential risks. We discuss different types of insurance, including health insurance, life insurance, home insurance, and auto insurance, and highlight the importance of assessing individual needs and coverage options. By understanding the risks we face and having appropriate insurance coverage in place, readers can protect their financial well-being and guard against unforeseen events.

Estate Planning: Ensuring a Smooth Wealth Transition
Estate planning is essential for individuals who wish to pass on their wealth and assets to future generations. This section delves into the

components of estate planning, including wills, trusts, power of attorney, and healthcare directives. We discuss the importance of defining beneficiaries, minimizing estate taxes, and establishing clear instructions for the distribution of assets. By engaging in thoughtful estate planning, readers can ensure a smooth transition of their wealth and legacy, providing financial stability and support for their loved ones.

Chapter 3: Cultivating a Wealth Mindset: Harnessing the Power of Abundance

Introduction:
In this chapter, we delve deep into the mindset and attitudes that are essential for building wealth and achieving financial success. The way we think about money, abundance, and opportunities greatly influences our financial outcomes. By adopting a wealth mindset, readers can unlock their potential, overcome limiting beliefs, and embrace a mindset that attracts prosperity. Through a combination of self-belief, positive thinking, and strategic action, readers can cultivate a mindset that paves the way for financial abundance.

Section 1: Shifting Your Money Mindset
1.1 The Power of Belief: Recognizing the Influence of Thoughts
Our thoughts have a profound impact on our beliefs, actions, and ultimately, our financial outcomes. In this section, we explore the power of belief and how our thoughts shape our reality. We delve into the concept of self-limiting beliefs, those deeply ingrained convictions that hold us back from achieving our true potential. By recognizing and challenging negative beliefs about money, readers can shift their mindset and open themselves up to new opportunities and possibilities.

1.2 Embracing an Abundance Mentality: Seeing Opportunities Everywhere

Abundance mentality is a transformative mindset that involves seeing the world as full of opportunities and possibilities. In this section, we delve into the power of positive thinking, gratitude, and reframing perspectives. By adopting an abundance mindset, readers can cultivate a deep sense of gratitude for what they have, focus on possibilities rather than limitations, and attract wealth and abundance into their lives.

1.3 Rewiring Your Money Story: Transforming Limiting Financial Narratives

Our past experiences and narratives shape our relationship with money. In this section, we explore the process of rewriting our money stories, letting go of limiting beliefs, and reframing our financial experiences. By examining the narratives we've held onto, we can identify patterns that have held us back and replace them with empowering stories of growth, abundance, and success. By cultivating a positive and empowering money narrative, readers can transform their relationship with money and create a new foundation for financial success.

Section 2: Developing Financial Confidence

2.1 Building Self-Confidence: Overcoming Financial Fears and Doubts

Confidence is a key attribute for achieving financial success. In this section, we dive into strategies for building self-confidence in the realm of finance. We explore techniques such as setting achievable goals, embracing continuous learning, celebrating small victories, and nurturing a positive self-image. By developing a strong sense of self-confidence, readers can overcome financial fears and doubts, allowing them to take calculated risks, step out of their comfort zones, and seize opportunities.

2.2 Mastering Financial Literacy: Empowering Yourself with Knowledge

Financial literacy is the foundation of a wealth mindset. In this section, we emphasize the importance of understanding key financial concepts and principles. We delve into topics such as budgeting, saving, investing, debt management, and understanding financial markets. By empowering themselves with comprehensive financial knowledge, readers can make informed decisions, navigate the complexities of the financial world, and optimize their financial outcomes.

2.3 Surrounding Yourself with Positive Influences: Building a Supportive Network

The company we keep significantly impacts our mindset and beliefs. In this section, we discuss the importance of surrounding oneself with positive influences. We explore the benefits of seeking mentors, finding role models, connecting with like-minded individuals, and joining supportive communities. By surrounding themselves with a supportive network, readers can draw inspiration, share experiences, receive guidance, and maintain a positive outlook on their wealth-building journey.

Section 3: Taking Strategic Action

3.1 Setting Clear Financial Goals: Creating a Roadmap for Success

Goal setting is the foundation of wealth creation. In this section, we explore the process of setting clear and achievable financial goals. We delve into techniques for clarifying one's vision, identifying specific objectives, and breaking them down into manageable steps. By setting well-defined goals, readers can create a roadmap for their financial success, maintain focus, and track their progress.

3.2 Designing a Personalized Wealth Building Plan: Strategies for Financial Success

Having a well-crafted plan is crucial for effective wealth building. In this section, we discuss the elements of a personalized wealth building plan. We explore various strategies such as creating multiple income streams, diversifying investments, managing cash flow, and maximizing tax advantages. By designing a tailored plan, readers can optimize their financial resources, mitigate risks, and accelerate their wealth-building journey.

3.3 Taking Consistent Action: Implementing Habits for Financial Success

Taking consistent action is key to turning financial goals into tangible results. In this section, we explore the importance of developing positive financial habits and rituals. We discuss the power of discipline, time management, and prioritization. By implementing daily actions aligned with their financial goals, readers can establish positive habits that lead to long-term success.

Section 4: Navigating Investment Strategies

4.1 Understanding Investment Basics: An Introduction to Different Asset Classes

Investing is a fundamental component of wealth building. In this section, we provide an overview of various asset classes, including stocks, bonds, real estate, and alternative investments. We discuss their characteristics, potential risks and returns, and the role they play in a diversified investment portfolio. By understanding the basics of each asset class, readers can make informed investment decisions aligned with their financial goals.

4.2 Building a Diversified Investment Portfolio: Spreading Risk and Maximizing Returns

Diversification is a key strategy for managing investment risk and optimizing returns. In this section, we delve into the importance of building a diversified investment portfolio. We explore techniques such as asset allocation, rebalancing, and considering investment horizons. By diversifying their investment holdings across different asset classes and sectors, readers can reduce their exposure to risk and enhance their long-term investment performance.

4.3 Assessing Risk Tolerance: Aligning Investments with Personal Comfort

Understanding one's risk tolerance is crucial for making appropriate investment decisions. In this section, we discuss the concept of risk tolerance and its significance in determining investment strategies. We explore various factors that influence risk tolerance, such as financial goals, time horizon, and personal circumstances. By aligning investments with their risk tolerance level, readers can build a portfolio that balances potential returns with their comfort level.

Section 5: Exploring Business Ideas
5.1 Identifying Opportunities: Discovering Business Ideas in the Market
Entrepreneurship presents an avenue for wealth creation. In this section, we discuss the process of identifying business opportunities in the market. We explore techniques for spotting trends, conducting market research, and recognizing unmet needs. By developing a keen eye for business opportunities, readers can tap into potential ventures that align with their skills, interests, and market demand.

5.2 Evaluating Business Viability: Assessing Feasibility and Market Potential
Once a business idea is identified, it's essential to evaluate its viability. In this section, we delve into the importance of assessing the feasibility and market potential of a business concept. We discuss methods for conducting market analysis, assessing competition, and evaluating financial projections. By critically evaluating the viability of their business ideas, readers can make informed decisions and increase their chances of entrepreneurial success.

5.3 Planning for Business Success: Strategies for Effective Business Management
Running a successful business requires careful planning and management. In this section, we explore key aspects of business planning and operations. We discuss topics such as creating a business plan, developing marketing strategies, managing finances, and building a strong team. By implementing effective business management strategies, readers can increase the likelihood of sustainable growth and profitability.

Chapter 4: Mastering Personal Finance: Strategies for Financial Stability and Growth

Introduction:
In this chapter, we dive into the realm of personal finance, exploring essential strategies for achieving financial stability, managing money effectively, and fostering long-term growth. By understanding the principles of personal finance and implementing sound financial practices, readers can take control of their financial well-being, make informed decisions, and lay the groundwork for a prosperous future.

Section 1: Budgeting and Cash Flow Management
1.1 The Importance of Budgeting: Creating a Blueprint for Financial Success
Budgeting is the cornerstone of effective financial management. In this section, we emphasize the significance of creating a budget and tracking income and expenses. We explore techniques for setting financial goals, categorizing expenses, and allocating funds wisely. By creating a well-defined budget, readers can gain clarity on their financial situation, identify areas for improvement, and make informed spending decisions.

1.2 Strategies for Effective Expense Management: Saving and Cutting Costs
Managing expenses is a vital aspect of personal finance. In this section, we delve into strategies for effective expense management. We discuss techniques for saving money, reducing discretionary spending, negotiating bills, and optimizing everyday expenses. By adopting frugal habits and making conscious spending choices,

readers can maximize their savings potential and allocate resources towards their financial goals.

1.3 Managing Cash Flow: Maintaining a Healthy Financial Balance
Cash flow management is crucial for financial stability. In this section, we explore techniques for managing income and expenses to maintain a healthy financial balance. We discuss the importance of tracking cash flow, building emergency funds, managing debt, and aligning expenses with income. By mastering cash flow management, readers can avoid financial stress, maintain liquidity, and make proactive financial decisions.

Section 2: Debt Management and Credit
2.1 Understanding Debt: Types, Risks, and Strategies
Debt management is vital for maintaining a strong financial foundation. In this section, we provide an overview of different types of debt, such as credit card debt, student loans, and mortgages. We discuss the risks associated with debt and explore strategies for effective debt management, including debt consolidation, prioritizing high-interest debt, and negotiating repayment terms. By understanding the nuances of debt and implementing smart repayment strategies, readers can reduce their financial burden and pave the way for future financial success.

2.2 Building and Maintaining a Healthy Credit Score
A good credit score is essential for accessing favorable financial opportunities. In this section, we explore the importance of credit scores, how they are calculated, and how to build and maintain a healthy credit history. We discuss techniques for improving credit scores, such as paying bills on time, managing credit utilization, and monitoring credit reports. By establishing and nurturing a positive credit history, readers can unlock better loan terms, lower interest rates, and improved financial flexibility.

2.3 Smart Credit Card Usage: Maximizing Rewards and Minimizing Risks

Credit cards can be powerful financial tools if used wisely. In this section, we delve into strategies for smart credit card usage. We discuss techniques for maximizing rewards, managing balances, avoiding unnecessary fees, and protecting against fraud. By understanding the benefits and risks of credit cards and adopting responsible credit card practices, readers can leverage these tools to their advantage while safeguarding their financial well-being.

Section 3: Building an Emergency Fund and Saving for the Future
3.1 The Importance of an Emergency Fund: Financial Safety Net for Unforeseen Circumstances
An emergency fund is crucial for financial resilience. In this section, we emphasize the significance of building an emergency fund. We discuss the recommended amount to save, strategies for building the fund, and the role it plays in protecting against unexpected expenses or income disruptions. By prioritizing and consistently contributing to an emergency fund, readers can mitigate the impact of unforeseen circumstances and maintain financial stability.

3.2 Strategies for Effective Saving: Setting Goals and Establishing Saving Habits
Saving is a key element of financial success. In this section, we explore strategies for effective saving. We discuss techniques for setting savings goals, automating savings contributions, and developing a saving mindset. By adopting proactive saving habits and aligning saving practices with their financial goals, readers can accumulate wealth, fund their dreams, and build a solid financial foundation.

3.3 Investing for the Future: Strategies for Long-Term Wealth Accumulation
Investing is a vital component of building wealth over the long term. In this section, we introduce readers to the world of investing. We discuss the benefits of investing, different investment options, and strategies for selecting suitable investments based on risk tolerance and financial goals. By understanding the fundamentals of investing and developing a well-rounded investment strategy, readers can

harness the power of compounding returns and accelerate their journey towards financial independence.

Chapter 5: Exploring Investment Opportunities: Strategies for Building Wealth

Section 1: Stocks and Equities
1.1 Understanding Stocks: Ownership in Profitable Companies
In this section, we introduce the concept of stocks and equities. Stocks represent ownership in profitable companies and provide investors with the potential for capital appreciation and dividend income. We discuss the basics of stock ownership, such as common stocks and preferred stocks, and how they trade in the stock market. We also explore the importance of conducting thorough research and analysis before investing in individual stocks.

1.2 Fundamental Analysis: Evaluating the Financial Health of Companies
Fundamental analysis is a critical tool for assessing the value and potential of individual stocks. In this section, we delve deeper into the process of evaluating the financial health of companies. We discuss techniques for analyzing financial statements, assessing earnings growth potential, and considering industry trends. We also explore the concept of intrinsic value and how it guides investment decisions. By mastering fundamental analysis, readers can make informed investment decisions and identify undervalued stocks with growth potential.

1.3 Technical Analysis: Analyzing Market Trends and Patterns

Technical analysis involves studying historical price and volume data to predict future price movements. In this section, we explore the principles of technical analysis and its application in stock investing. We discuss various technical indicators, chart patterns, and trend analysis techniques. By incorporating technical analysis into their investment approach, readers can gain insights into market sentiment and make well-timed investment decisions. We emphasize the importance of combining fundamental and technical analysis for a comprehensive investment strategy.

Section 2: Bonds and Fixed-Income Investments
2.1 Understanding Bonds: Loaning Money to Governments and Corporations
Bonds are debt instruments that provide fixed income to investors. In this section, we provide a detailed understanding of bonds and their role in fixed-income investing. We discuss different types of bonds, such as government bonds, corporate bonds, and municipal bonds, and explore their risk and return characteristics. We also explain how bond prices and yields are determined and the influence of interest rates and credit ratings.

2.2 Evaluating Bond Investments: Assessing Credit Risk and Yield Potential
When investing in bonds, it's crucial to evaluate credit risk and yield potential. In this section, we discuss techniques for assessing the creditworthiness of bond issuers, analyzing bond ratings, and understanding yield-to-maturity. We explore the relationship between bond prices and interest rates, as well as the impact of inflation on bond investments. We also delve into strategies for diversifying bond investments and managing interest rate risk. By conducting thorough due diligence, readers can make informed decisions and construct a balanced fixed-income portfolio.

2.3 Bond Strategies: Building a Fixed-Income Portfolio
Building a successful fixed-income portfolio requires careful consideration of bond strategies. In this section, we explore different approaches to constructing a fixed-income portfolio based on

investment objectives and risk tolerance. We discuss strategies such as laddering, barbelling, and bullet portfolios. We also explore the role of bond mutual funds and exchange-traded funds (ETFs) in accessing diversified bond exposure. By understanding bond strategies, readers can optimize their fixed-income investments and achieve their financial goals.

Section 3: Real Estate and Property Investments
3.1 Exploring Real Estate Investments: Generating Income and Building Equity
Real estate investments offer opportunities for income generation and capital appreciation. In this section, we delve into the different avenues for investing in real estate. We discuss residential properties, commercial properties, real estate investment trusts (REITs), and real estate crowdfunding. We explore the benefits and risks associated with each option and provide insights into market trends and property valuation.

3.2 Rental Properties: Assessing Cash Flow and Property Management
Investing in rental properties requires a comprehensive understanding of cash flow and effective property management. In this section, we discuss techniques for analyzing rental property cash flow, including rental income, expenses, and vacancy rates. We delve into the importance of property location, market demand, and tenant screening. We also explore strategies for property management, maintenance, and leveraging financing options. By understanding the nuances of rental property investing, readers can build a sustainable income stream and grow their real estate portfolio.

3.3 Commercial Real Estate: Opportunities and Risks
Commercial real estate offers unique investment opportunities and challenges. In this section, we explore different types of commercial properties, such as office buildings, retail centers, and industrial properties. We discuss the factors influencing commercial real estate investments, including lease agreements, property valuation

methods, and economic cycles. We also examine the potential risks and rewards associated with commercial real estate investing and highlight key considerations for success.

Section 4: Alternative Investments and Diversification
4.1 Exploring Alternative Investments: Beyond Stocks and Bonds
Alternative investments provide opportunities for diversification and potential uncorrelated returns. In this section, we introduce readers to various alternative investment options. We discuss commodities, precious metals, hedge funds, private equity, venture capital, and cryptocurrencies. We explore the benefits, risks, and considerations associated with each alternative investment and how they can complement a well-diversified portfolio.

4.2 Diversification Strategies: Spreading Risk and Maximizing Returns
Diversification is key to managing investment risk and maximizing returns. In this section, we delve into diversification strategies for building a well-balanced investment portfolio. We discuss asset allocation, portfolio rebalancing, and the importance of spreading investments across different asset classes and sectors. We explore the concept of risk management and how to assess risk tolerance. By implementing effective diversification strategies, readers can reduce their exposure to individual investment risks and achieve more stable and consistent returns.

Chapter 6: Entrepreneurship and Small Business Ventures

:

Section 1: The Entrepreneurial Mindset

1.1 The Spirit of Entrepreneurship: Embracing Innovation and Risk-Taking

Entrepreneurship is a magnificent blend of innovation, creativity, and a daring willingness to take calculated risks. In this section, we dive into the core of a successful entrepreneur's mindset. We explore the importance of embracing change, thinking outside the box, and challenging the status quo. We delve into the depths of curiosity, resilience, and the insatiable thirst for continuous learning. By adopting an entrepreneurial mindset, readers can develop the necessary traits to navigate the challenges and seize remarkable opportunities in the dynamic world of business.

1.2 Identifying Business Opportunities: Market Research and Analysis

Astute entrepreneurs possess a keen eye for spotting lucrative business opportunities. In this section, we embark on an exhilarating journey into the realm of market research and analysis. We unveil powerful techniques for understanding customer needs, analyzing market trends, and evaluating competition. We emphasize the significance of conducting comprehensive feasibility studies and validating business ideas before committing precious resources. By honing their market research skills, readers can unlock the door to remarkable business opportunities and position themselves for extraordinary success.

1.3 The Power of Networking: Building Meaningful Relationships and Partnerships

Networking is the lifeblood of entrepreneurship, opening doors to invaluable relationships and strategic partnerships. In this section, we unravel the art of networking and relationship-building. We reveal the secrets to expanding professional networks, attending industry events, and leveraging the potential of social media platforms. We delve into the profound benefits of collaborating with like-minded individuals, wise mentors, and industry experts. By nurturing a robust network, readers can tap into a boundless reservoir of knowledge, support, and awe-inspiring business opportunities.

Section 2: Business Planning and Strategy

2.1 Crafting a Business Plan: Vision, Mission, and Objectives

A well-crafted business plan serves as a guiding light on the arduous path to entrepreneurial success. In this section, we embark on a meticulous exploration of the components that constitute a comprehensive business plan. We emphasize the utmost importance of defining a clear vision, a compelling mission statement, and strategic objectives. We unveil techniques for conducting a thorough SWOT analysis (Strengths, Weaknesses, Opportunities, Threats), defining target markets, and outlining ingenious marketing and sales strategies. By developing a rock-solid business plan, readers can articulate their business vision with extraordinary precision and chart a course for remarkable decision-making.

2.2 Financial Planning and Funding: Budgeting and Capital Acquisition

Financial planning is the lifeblood of entrepreneurial endeavors. In this section, we immerse ourselves in the intricacies of creating a robust financial plan for a new business. We unveil techniques for meticulous budgeting, astute cash flow management, and accurate financial projections. We explore the diverse array of funding sources available, including personal savings, loans, venture capital, and the transformative power of crowdfunding. We underscore the paramount importance of understanding financial statements and seeking professional advice when navigating complex financial terrain. By mastering the art of financial planning, readers can deftly manage their business finances and secure the vital capital necessary for unprecedented growth.

2.3 Developing a Competitive Advantage: Differentiation and Value Proposition

In a fiercely competitive business landscape, the development of a unique value proposition and a compelling competitive advantage is paramount. In this section, we delve into the captivating strategies for differentiating a business and carving out a prominent market position. We unveil the secrets of identifying target customer segments, empathetically understanding their needs, and ingeniously delivering products or services that surpass expectations. We explore techniques for branding, skillful positioning, and the art of building an indomitable brand identity. By developing an irresistible value proposition, readers can magnetize customers, outperform competitors, and catapult their businesses to unparalleled heights of success.

Section 3: Managing and Growing a Small Business
3.1 Effective Leadership and Team Building: Inspiring and Empowering Others
In the realm of entrepreneurship, exceptional leadership and team-building skills are indispensable. In this section, we embark on an illuminating exploration of the qualities that define remarkable leaders and the strategies that foster the formation of high-performing teams. We delve into the profound importance of crystal-clear communication, purposeful delegation, and the nurturing of a harmonious work culture. We unveil techniques for motivating and empowering employees, recognizing their invaluable contributions, and fostering a collaborative environment that ignites creativity and fuels productivity. By mastering the art of leadership and team building, readers can create a flourishing workplace that propels their business toward unprecedented success.

3.2 Operations Management: Efficiency, Productivity, and Quality Control
Efficient operations management lies at the heart of organizational excellence, optimizing productivity and maintaining impeccable quality standards. In this section, we embark on a transformative journey into the intricacies of streamlining business operations, optimizing processes, and igniting a culture of continuous improvement. We delve into the secrets of effective inventory management, supply chain optimization, and the fine art of embracing cutting-edge technology to unlock operational efficiencies. We emphasize the pivotal role of quality control and unwavering customer satisfaction in propelling businesses toward

unrivaled triumph. By implementing astute operations management strategies, readers can supercharge productivity, slash costs, and deliver exquisite products or services that mesmerize customers.

3.3 Marketing and Sales Strategies: Reaching Customers and Fueling Growth
Marketing and sales strategies are the lifeblood of business success, propelling entrepreneurs toward the pinnacle of achievement. In this section, we dive into the captivating techniques and strategies that galvanize customer interest and drive business growth. We explore the profound significance of market segmentation, skillful targeting, and artful positioning to captivate the hearts and minds of the target audience. We unveil the transformative power of digital marketing, social media advertising, compelling content creation, and the art of nurturing enduring customer relationships. We emphasize the importance of measuring marketing effectiveness, harnessing the power of data-driven insights, and adapting strategies to ever-evolving market trends. By implementing astute marketing and sales strategies, readers can magnetize their target audience, foster brand loyalty, and unlock a river of revenue.

Chapter 7: Financial Intelligence: Building Wealth through Strategic Investments

Section 1: The Foundations of Financial Intelligence

1.1 The Power of Financial Education: Empowering Yourself with Knowledge
Financial intelligence begins with a solid foundation of knowledge and understanding. In this section, we explore the significance of financial education and the transformative impact it can have on one's financial journey. We discuss the importance of learning about key financial concepts such as budgeting, saving, investing, and understanding financial markets. We delve into the importance of developing a growth mindset, seeking out reputable resources, and continuously expanding one's financial knowledge. By equipping themselves with financial education, readers can navigate the complex world of finance with confidence and make sound investment decisions.

1.2 Setting Financial Goals: Mapping Your Path to Success
Goal-setting is a crucial step in achieving financial success. In this section, we explore the art of setting meaningful and achievable financial goals. We discuss the importance of defining short-term and long-term goals, understanding personal aspirations, and aligning financial objectives with one's values and priorities. We delve into techniques for creating a financial roadmap, breaking down goals into actionable steps, and tracking progress along the way. By setting clear financial goals, readers can stay focused, motivated, and on track toward building substantial wealth.

1.3 Understanding Risk and Reward: The Balancing Act of Investment
Investment inherently involves risk, but it also presents opportunities for substantial rewards. In this section, we dive into the delicate balance of risk and reward in investment decisions. We explore different types of investments, including stocks, bonds, real estate, and mutual funds. We discuss the concept of diversification and its role in mitigating risk. We delve into the importance of conducting thorough research, analyzing market trends, and seeking professional advice when making investment decisions. By understanding the dynamics of risk and reward, readers can make

informed investment choices that align with their financial goals and risk tolerance.

Section 2: Building Wealth through Strategic Investments
2.1 Investment Strategies: Long-Term Thinking and Smart Portfolio Management
Building wealth requires a strategic approach to investment. In this section, we explore different investment strategies and the principles that guide successful portfolio management. We discuss the significance of long-term thinking, patience, and disciplined investing. We delve into the concept of asset allocation, balancing risk and return, and adjusting investment portfolios as circumstances evolve. We emphasize the importance of diversifying investments across different asset classes and industries. By adopting sound investment strategies, readers can position themselves for long-term wealth accumulation and financial security.

2.2 Real Estate Investment: Unlocking the Power of Property Ownership
Real estate investment can be a powerful vehicle for wealth creation. In this section, we delve into the intricacies of real estate investment, including rental properties, commercial real estate, and real estate investment trusts (REITs). We discuss the advantages and challenges of investing in real estate, including property valuation, market analysis, financing options, and property management. We explore strategies for identifying lucrative real estate opportunities, maximizing rental income, and leveraging appreciation. By understanding the dynamics of real estate investment, readers can tap into the potential of property ownership as a means to build substantial wealth.

2.3 Entrepreneurship and Business Ventures: Investments in Innovation and Growth
Entrepreneurship and business ventures offer unique investment opportunities. In this section, we explore the world of investing in startups, small businesses, and innovative ventures. We discuss the potential for high returns and the risks associated with investing in

early-stage companies. We delve into the importance of conducting thorough due diligence, assessing market potential, and understanding the business model before investing. We explore strategies for evaluating investment opportunities, negotiating deals, and managing risks. By embracing the world of entrepreneurship and business investments, readers can participate in the growth of innovative ventures and potentially reap substantial financial rewards.

Chapter 8: The Art of Saving and Budgeting: Maximizing Your Financial Resources

Introduction:
In this chapter, we delve into the art of saving and budgeting, essential skills for building wealth and managing personal finances effectively. We explore the importance of saving money, developing a budgeting system, and making conscious financial choices that align with your goals. By mastering the art of saving and budgeting, readers can maximize their financial resources, create a strong financial foundation, and take control of their financial future.

Section 1: The Power of Saving Money
1.1 The Benefits of Saving: Creating Financial Security and Freedom
Saving money is a fundamental aspect of financial success. In this section, we explore the various benefits of saving, including building an emergency fund, creating a safety net, and having resources for future investments. We discuss the peace of mind that comes with financial security and the freedom that saving provides to pursue opportunities and weather unforeseen circumstances. We provide practical tips on how to develop a saving mindset and overcome common obstacles to saving.

1.2 Strategies for Saving: Setting Goals and Implementing Effective Techniques

Saving requires discipline and a strategic approach. In this section, we delve into strategies for saving money, including setting clear financial goals, creating a budget, and automating savings. We discuss the importance of tracking expenses, identifying areas of unnecessary spending, and making conscious choices to prioritize saving. We provide practical tips and techniques for reducing expenses, negotiating bills, and finding ways to save on everyday purchases.

1.3 Building a Solid Emergency Fund: Safeguarding Against Financial Uncertainty

An emergency fund is a crucial component of financial stability. In this section, we explore the importance of building an emergency fund and discuss how to determine the appropriate amount based on individual circumstances. We delve into strategies for saving for emergencies, such as creating a dedicated savings account, setting up automatic transfers, and gradually increasing the fund over time. We emphasize the peace of mind that comes with having a safety net to handle unexpected expenses or income disruptions. Additionally, we provide insights on how to grow the emergency fund through wise investment choices and maximizing returns.

1.4 Harnessing the Power of Compound Interest: Growing Your Wealth Over Time

Compound interest is a powerful force that can significantly impact wealth accumulation. In this section, we explain the concept of compound interest and how it can work in your favor when saving and investing. We delve into the magic of compounding returns and illustrate its impact over different time horizons. We provide practical examples and strategies for harnessing the power of compound interest, such as investing in tax-advantaged retirement accounts, diversifying investments, and reinvesting dividends. By understanding the power of compound interest, readers can unlock the potential to accelerate their wealth-building journey.

Section 2: Mastering the Art of Budgeting

2.1 The Benefits of Budgeting: Gaining Control and Making Informed Financial Decisions

Budgeting is a powerful tool for managing personal finances. In this section, we explore the benefits of budgeting, including gaining control over spending habits, tracking income and expenses, and making informed financial decisions. We discuss how budgeting can help prioritize financial goals, reduce debt, and plan for the future. We provide insights on the positive impact budgeting can have on overall financial well-being, including stress reduction and improved financial security.

2.2 Creating a Personal Budget: Developing a Financial Roadmap

Developing a personal budget is the cornerstone of effective financial management. In this section, we guide readers through the process of creating a budget, starting with identifying income sources and understanding fixed and variable expenses. We discuss different budgeting methods, such as the 50/30/20 rule, envelope system, or budgeting apps, and how to choose the approach that aligns with individual preferences. We provide tips for tracking expenses, monitoring progress, and making adjustments to the budget as needed. Additionally, we explore advanced budgeting techniques, such as zero-based budgeting and cash flow forecasting, for those seeking to fine-tune their budgeting skills.

2.3 Managing Debt: Strategies for Debt Repayment and Avoidance

Debt can hinder financial progress, but with a solid budgeting plan, it can be effectively managed and ultimately eliminated. In this section, we explore strategies for managing debt, including prioritizing debt repayment, negotiating lower interest rates, and consolidating debts. We provide insights on avoiding unnecessary debt and making informed borrowing decisions. We discuss the importance of building a positive credit history and maintaining a healthy debt-to-income ratio. Furthermore, we provide guidance on strategies for accelerating debt repayment, such as the debt snowball method and debt avalanche method, empowering readers to take control of their financial obligations.

2.4 Building Wealth Through Strategic Saving and Investing
Saving alone is not enough to build long-term wealth. In this section, we explore how strategic saving and investing can help readers grow their wealth over time. We discuss different investment vehicles, including stocks, bonds, mutual funds, real estate, and retirement accounts. We provide insights on diversification, asset allocation, and risk management to help readers make informed investment decisions. We also address common investment pitfalls and provide guidance on how to avoid scams and fraudulent schemes. By understanding the principles of strategic saving and investing, readers can lay the foundation for long-term wealth accumulation and financial security.

Section 1: The Power of Saving Money

1.1 The Benefits of Saving: Creating Financial Security and Freedom

Savings play a pivotal role in achieving financial security and freedom. By diligently setting aside a portion of your income, you can build a safety net that protects you from unexpected expenses, income fluctuations, and future uncertainties. Let's delve deeper into the various benefits of saving and explore why it is a crucial aspect of your financial journey.

First and foremost, saving money provides a sense of security and peace of mind. Life is full of surprises, and having savings allows you to tackle unexpected situations with confidence. Whether it's a sudden medical expense, a car repair, or an unforeseen job loss, having a financial buffer can alleviate the stress and anxiety that accompany these circumstances. With savings, you can face such challenges head-on, knowing that you have the necessary funds to handle them without resorting to high-interest loans or credit card debt.

Moreover, savings grant you the freedom to make choices that align with your long-term goals. It empowers you to pursue opportunities without being bound by financial constraints. Want to start your own business? Save for a down payment on a home? Take a sabbatical to travel and explore the world? With sufficient savings, you can turn these dreams into reality. By consistently setting aside money, you create a financial cushion that enables you to make intentional decisions, explore new ventures, and live life on your terms.

In addition to providing security and freedom, saving money allows you to weather income fluctuations and economic downturns. It serves as a buffer during periods of reduced income or unexpected financial hardships. By having savings, you can bridge the gap and maintain your standard of living even when faced with temporary financial challenges. This provides a sense of stability and allows you to focus on finding new income opportunities or weathering the storm until better times arrive.

Furthermore, saving money also enables you to take advantage of future investment opportunities. Investments can provide avenues for your money to grow and generate passive income. Whether it's investing in the stock market, real estate, or starting a business, having savings puts you in a position to capitalize on these opportunities. By setting aside funds for investments, you can diversify your financial portfolio and potentially build wealth over time.

Moreover, savings provide a sense of financial independence. It grants you the freedom to break free from the paycheck-to-paycheck cycle and achieve financial stability. By cultivating disciplined saving habits, you can gradually reduce reliance on credit and debt, and instead, rely on your own resources. This independence empowers you to make informed financial decisions, seize opportunities that align with your values and aspirations, and create a more secure and prosperous future for yourself and your loved ones.

Section 1.2: The Habit of Saving: Building Financial Discipline

In addition to the numerous benefits of saving money, developing the habit of saving is equally important. Building financial discipline and cultivating a savings mindset can have a profound impact on your long-term financial well-being. Let's explore the key elements of developing the habit of saving and how it can contribute to your financial success.

Start Small and Be Consistent: Saving money is not about the amount you save initially, but about establishing a consistent habit. Begin by setting aside a small portion of your income, even if it's just a few dollars each week. The key is to be consistent in your savings efforts, making it a priority each time you receive income. Over time, these small savings will accumulate and grow into a substantial amount.

Automate Your Savings: One effective way to ensure consistent savings is to automate the process. Set up automatic transfers from your checking account to a designated savings account. By automating your savings, you remove the temptation to spend the money before saving it. Treat saving as a regular expense, just like paying your bills, and make it a non-negotiable part of your financial routine.

Create a Budget: Developing a budget is essential for managing your finances effectively and identifying areas where you can save. Take the time to analyze your income and expenses, and allocate a specific portion towards savings. By having a clear understanding of your financial inflows and outflows, you can make informed decisions about how much you can comfortably save each month.

Set Savings Goals: Establishing specific savings goals provides a sense of purpose and motivation. Whether it's saving for a down payment on a house, a dream vacation, or an emergency fund, having clear objectives helps you stay focused on your savings journey. Break down your goals into smaller milestones and track your progress regularly. Celebrate each milestone achieved, which will further fuel your motivation to continue saving.

Cut Expenses and Prioritize: Take a close look at your expenses and identify areas where you can cut back. This could involve reducing discretionary spending, finding more affordable alternatives for everyday items, or renegotiating bills and subscriptions. Prioritize your spending based on what truly aligns with your values and long-term goals. By making conscious choices about where your money goes, you free up additional funds to allocate towards savings.

Stay Disciplined and Resist Temptation: Saving money requires discipline and the ability to resist immediate gratification. Understand the difference between needs and wants, and prioritize your long-term financial well-being over short-term impulses. Practice delayed gratification by resisting unnecessary purchases and focusing on the bigger picture.

In conclusion, developing the habit of saving is a foundational step towards financial success. Start small, be consistent, and automate your savings to make it a seamless part of your financial routine. Create a budget, set savings goals, cut expenses, and stay disciplined. Remember, building financial discipline is not an overnight process, but with time and persistence, it becomes a natural part of your financial habits. Embrace the power of saving and watch your wealth grow over time.

Section 1.3: Maximizing Your Savings: Strategies for Accelerated Growth

While saving money is essential, maximizing your savings can accelerate your path to financial success. By implementing effective strategies, you can optimize your savings potential and achieve your financial goals more efficiently. Let's explore some strategies for maximizing your savings and accelerating your wealth-building journey.

Embrace Frugality: Frugality is a mindset that focuses on making intentional choices to minimize expenses and maximize savings. Embrace a frugal lifestyle by adopting practices such as meal planning, buying in bulk, and seeking out discounts and deals. Look for ways to reduce unnecessary expenses and prioritize value over frivolous spending. By being mindful of your spending habits, you can free up more money to allocate towards savings.

Increase Your Income: While saving is crucial, increasing your income can provide a significant boost to your savings potential. Explore opportunities to grow your income, such as taking on side gigs or freelance work, pursuing career advancement, or starting a part-time business. Invest in acquiring new skills and knowledge that can lead to higher-paying job opportunities. By expanding your earning potential, you can allocate a larger portion of your income towards savings.

Leverage Tax-Advantaged Accounts: Take advantage of tax-advantaged accounts, such as 401(k) plans, Individual Retirement Accounts (IRAs), or Health Savings Accounts (HSAs). These accounts offer tax benefits that can help your savings grow faster. Contribute the maximum amount allowed to these accounts and consider employer matching programs to maximize your contributions. By reducing your tax liability and benefiting from compounding growth, you can accelerate the growth of your savings.

Explore High-Yield Savings Options: Traditional savings accounts may offer minimal interest rates. Explore high-yield savings accounts or certificates of deposit (CDs) that provide higher interest rates on your savings. Research online banks and financial institutions to find the best rates available. While these options may have certain limitations, they can help your savings grow at a faster pace compared to traditional savings accounts.

Invest Wisely: Consider investing a portion of your savings in vehicles that have the potential for higher returns. Diversify your investment portfolio with a mix of stocks, bonds, mutual funds, or real estate, depending on your risk tolerance and financial goals. Educate yourself about different investment options and seek professional advice if needed. Investing wisely can provide the opportunity for your savings to grow significantly over the long term.

Review and Adjust: Regularly review your savings strategy and make adjustments as necessary. Life circumstances and financial goals may change, requiring modifications to your savings approach. Stay informed about market trends, interest rates, and new savings opportunities. Continually assess your budget, expenses, and income to ensure you're maximizing your savings potential.

Section 1.4: Overcoming Savings Challenges: Strategies for Success

Saving money is not without its challenges. It requires discipline, perseverance, and the ability to overcome obstacles along the way. In this section, we will explore common savings challenges and provide strategies to help you overcome them, ensuring your path to financial success remains on track.

Temptation and Impulse Spending: One of the biggest challenges to saving is the temptation to indulge in impulse purchases. The allure of immediate gratification can undermine your savings efforts. To overcome this challenge, practice self-control and delay gratification. Before making a purchase, ask yourself if it aligns with your long-term goals. Implement a waiting period before buying non-essential items, allowing yourself time to evaluate the necessity and prioritize your savings.

Lifestyle Inflation: As your income increases, it's common for spending to increase as well, often leading to lifestyle inflation. This can hinder your savings progress. Avoid falling into the trap of increasing expenses in line with your income. Instead, maintain a modest lifestyle and direct the additional income towards savings and investments. Keep your long-term goals in mind and resist the urge to upgrade your lifestyle unnecessarily.

Unexpected Expenses: Life is full of surprises, and unexpected expenses can derail your savings plans. To overcome this challenge, establish an emergency fund. Set aside three to six months' worth of living expenses in a separate savings account. This fund acts as a safety net, providing financial stability in times of unforeseen circumstances. Regularly contribute to your emergency fund, ensuring it is replenished after each use.

Debt Repayment: High levels of debt can impede your ability to save effectively. Prioritize debt repayment to alleviate the burden and free up more funds for savings. Implement a debt repayment plan, focusing on high-interest debts first. Consider debt consolidation options or negotiate with creditors to reduce interest rates or establish more favorable repayment terms. As you eliminate debt, redirect the money previously allocated to debt payments towards your savings.

Lack of Accountability: Lack of accountability can hinder your savings progress. It's essential to hold yourself accountable for your financial decisions and commitments. Consider finding an accountability partner, such as a trusted friend or family member, who can support and motivate you in your savings journey. Share your goals and progress regularly to stay on track. Additionally, track your expenses and savings diligently, using budgeting tools or apps to monitor your financial activities.

Lack of Financial Education: Limited financial knowledge can hinder effective savings strategies. Invest in your financial education by reading books, attending workshops, or seeking guidance from financial professionals. Educate yourself about personal finance, investment options, and money management. The more you understand about finances, the better equipped you'll be to make informed decisions and optimize your savings.

Section 2.1: Setting Financial Goals: The Foundation of Wealth-Building

Setting clear financial goals is crucial for effective wealth-building and financial management. Without a roadmap, it's challenging to make progress and measure your success. In this section, we will explore the importance of setting financial goals and provide strategies to help you define and achieve them.

Reflect on Your Values and Aspirations: Start by reflecting on your values and aspirations. What matters most to you in life? What are your long-term dreams and aspirations? Understanding your values and aligning your financial goals with them will provide a sense of purpose and motivation. Consider aspects such as family, career, lifestyle, education, retirement, and philanthropy. This reflection will lay the foundation for setting meaningful financial goals.

Define Specific and Measurable Goals: Vague goals are challenging to pursue. Instead, define specific and measurable goals that are clear and actionable. For example, instead of setting a general goal like "save more money," set a specific goal such as "save $10,000 in a high-yield savings account within the next year." This specific target provides clarity and allows you to track your progress effectively.

Set Short-Term and Long-Term Goals: It's essential to set both short-term and long-term financial goals. Short-term goals provide immediate milestones and a sense of accomplishment, while long-term goals keep you focused on the bigger picture. Identify goals that you can achieve within a few months to a year, as well as goals that span several years or even decades. By balancing short-term and long-term goals, you can maintain momentum and make progress towards your ultimate financial vision.

Make Goals Realistic and Attainable: While it's important to dream big, it's equally important to make your goals realistic and attainable. Consider your current financial situation, income, expenses, and time horizon. Set goals that stretch your capabilities but remain within reach. Unrealistic goals can lead to frustration and demotivation. Break down larger goals into smaller, achievable milestones to make them more manageable and celebrate your progress along the way.

Prioritize Your Goals: With multiple financial goals, it's crucial to prioritize them based on their importance and urgency. Determine which goals are most critical to your overall financial well-being and focus on those first. Consider the time sensitivity, potential impact, and alignment with your values when prioritizing. By allocating your resources and efforts to the most important goals, you can make significant strides towards achieving them.

Create an Action Plan: Once you have defined your financial goals, create a detailed action plan to guide your journey. Break down each goal into actionable steps and set deadlines for each milestone. Identify potential obstacles and develop strategies to overcome them. Regularly review and update your action plan as circumstances change. Having a well-defined roadmap will keep you on track and increase the likelihood of achieving your financial goals.

Section 2.2: Developing a Budget: Your Path to Financial Stability

A budget is a fundamental tool for managing your finances and achieving your financial goals. It provides a clear picture of your income, expenses, and savings, enabling you to make informed decisions and maintain financial stability. In this section, we will explore the importance of budgeting and provide practical steps to develop an effective budget.

Assess Your Current Financial Situation: Begin by assessing your current financial situation. Gather information about your income sources, including salaries, investments, and any other sources of revenue. Next, analyze your expenses, categorizing them into fixed (e.g., rent/mortgage, utilities) and variable (e.g., groceries, entertainment). Understanding your income and expenses will provide a baseline for developing your budget.

Determine Your Financial Priorities: With a clear understanding of your income and expenses, determine your financial priorities. Consider your short-term and long-term goals, such as saving for a down payment, paying off debt, or investing for retirement. By identifying your priorities, you can allocate your financial resources accordingly and ensure that your budget aligns with your goals.

Set Realistic Spending Targets: Setting realistic spending targets is crucial for effective budgeting. Evaluate your current expenses and identify areas where you can potentially reduce or optimize spending. Aim to strike a balance between your needs and wants, ensuring that your budget allows for both essential expenses and discretionary spending. Be realistic about your lifestyle and personal preferences, as overly restrictive budgets may be difficult to maintain over the long term.

Track Your Expenses: To develop an accurate budget, track your expenses diligently. Keep a record of all your purchases, either through a mobile app, spreadsheet, or a dedicated budgeting tool. Categorize your expenses and review them regularly to identify spending patterns and areas for improvement. By tracking your expenses, you can gain insights into your financial habits and make informed adjustments to your budget.

Allocate Your Income: Allocate your income based on your spending targets and financial priorities. Start by ensuring that your essential expenses, such as housing, utilities, and transportation, are covered. Then allocate funds towards savings and investments to achieve your long-term goals. Finally, set aside a portion of your income for discretionary spending and leisure activities. Remember to be flexible and adjust your allocations as needed to accommodate changes in income or expenses.

Review and Adjust Regularly: Budgeting is not a one-time activity but an ongoing process. Regularly review your budget to assess its effectiveness and make necessary adjustments. Analyze your actual spending against your budgeted amounts and identify any discrepancies or areas of improvement. Stay flexible and adapt your budget to changing circumstances, such as income fluctuations, new expenses, or unexpected events.

Seek Professional Guidance if Needed: If you find budgeting challenging or need assistance with complex financial situations, don't hesitate to seek professional guidance. Financial advisors or certified financial planners can provide valuable insights and help you develop a customized budgeting strategy that aligns with your goals and circumstances.

Section 2.3: Debt Management: Liberating Yourself from Financial Burdens

Debt can be a significant obstacle to financial well-being and wealth-building. Managing debt effectively is essential to regain control of your finances and work towards your financial goals. In this section, we will explore strategies for debt management and provide guidance on how to reduce debt and minimize its impact on your financial health.

Assess Your Debt Situation: Start by assessing your debt situation. Compile a list of all your outstanding debts, including credit cards, loans, and any other liabilities. Note the interest rates, minimum payments, and total balances for each debt. This assessment will give you a clear picture of your debt obligations and help you prioritize your repayment strategy.

Create a Debt Repayment Plan: Develop a comprehensive debt repayment plan to tackle your outstanding balances systematically. There are two common approaches: the snowball method and the avalanche method. The snowball method involves paying off debts with the smallest balances first, while the avalanche method focuses on debts with the highest interest rates. Choose the approach that aligns with your preferences and financial circumstances. Allocate a portion of your budget towards debt repayment and consistently make payments above the minimum required.

Negotiate with Creditors: In some cases, you may be able to negotiate with creditors to reduce interest rates, waive fees, or establish more manageable payment terms. Contact your creditors directly to explore these possibilities. Explain your financial situation and demonstrate your commitment to repaying the debt. While not all creditors may be willing to negotiate, it is worth exploring this option to potentially alleviate some financial burden.

Cut Expenses and Increase Income: To accelerate debt repayment, consider cutting expenses and finding ways to increase your income. Review your budget and identify areas where you can reduce discretionary spending. Explore cost-saving measures, such as cooking at home, canceling unnecessary subscriptions, or negotiating lower bills. Additionally, look for opportunities to increase your income, such as taking on a side gig, freelancing, or pursuing additional education to enhance your career prospects.

Prioritize High-Interest Debts: When allocating your resources towards debt repayment, prioritize high-interest debts. These debts accumulate more interest over time and can significantly impede your financial progress. By focusing on high-interest debts first, you minimize the amount of interest paid and expedite your journey to debt freedom.

Consider Debt Consolidation or Refinancing: Debt consolidation or refinancing may be viable options to simplify your debt management and potentially lower interest rates. Consolidating multiple debts into a single loan or transferring high-interest balances to lower-interest credit cards can make your debt more manageable. However, carefully evaluate the terms and fees associated with these options before proceeding.

Seek Professional Assistance: If your debt situation feels overwhelming or you need expert guidance, consider reaching out to credit counseling agencies or financial professionals. These professionals can provide personalized advice, help negotiate with creditors, and assist you in developing a tailored debt management plan.

Practice Responsible Credit Card Usage: To prevent accumulating further debt, practice responsible credit card usage. Pay off your credit card balances in full each month to avoid interest charges. Use credit cards for necessary expenses and emergencies rather than for frivolous purchases. Responsible credit card management will help you build a positive credit history and improve your overall financial health.

Section 2.4: Building an Emergency Fund: A Safety Net for Financial Stability

Life is full of unexpected events and financial emergencies. To safeguard your financial well-being, it is essential to establish an emergency fund. In this section, we will explore the importance of an emergency fund, how to build one, and the benefits it brings to your overall financial stability.

Understanding the Purpose of an Emergency Fund: An emergency fund serves as a safety net, providing you with a financial cushion to handle unexpected expenses or income disruptions. It serves as a buffer against job loss, medical emergencies, car repairs, or home repairs. By having an emergency fund, you can avoid resorting to high-interest debt or depleting your savings when faced with unforeseen circumstances.

Setting Your Emergency Fund Goal: Start by determining how much you should save in your emergency fund. A general rule of thumb is to aim for three to six months' worth of living expenses. However, this amount can vary depending on your personal circumstances. Consider factors such as job stability, family size, and specific financial responsibilities. Set a realistic goal that provides you with peace of mind and ensures you can comfortably cover your essential expenses during a financial setback.

Prioritizing Your Emergency Fund: Make your emergency fund a financial priority. Allocate a portion of your income specifically towards building and maintaining your emergency fund. Treat it as a non-negotiable expense, just like paying bills or saving for retirement. Consistently contribute to your emergency fund until you reach your desired savings goal.

Automate Your Savings: One effective strategy for building an emergency fund is to automate your savings. Set up an automatic transfer from your checking account to a separate savings account dedicated solely to your emergency fund. By automating this process, you remove the temptation to spend the money elsewhere and ensure consistent progress towards your goal.

Cut Expenses and Increase Savings: Accelerate your emergency fund growth by cutting unnecessary expenses and redirecting those savings towards your fund. Review your budget and identify areas where you can reduce discretionary spending. Consider eliminating non-essential subscriptions, dining out less frequently, or finding cost-effective alternatives for your daily expenses. By consciously reducing expenses, you free up more funds to contribute to your emergency fund.

Use Windfalls and Extra Income: Maximize your emergency fund growth by utilizing windfalls or extra income. Instead of spending unexpected bonuses, tax refunds, or monetary gifts, channel them directly into your emergency fund. This proactive approach helps you reach your savings goal faster and reinforces the importance of prioritizing financial stability.

Separate Your Emergency Fund from Regular Savings: To prevent accidental spending or confusion, keep your emergency fund separate from your regular savings. Open a dedicated savings account specifically for your emergency fund and avoid mixing it with other savings goals. This separation ensures that your emergency fund remains untouched unless a genuine emergency arises.

Replenish Your Fund After Use: If you dip into your emergency fund to cover unforeseen expenses, make it a priority to replenish it as soon as possible. Treat it as a loan to yourself and commit to repaying it diligently. Resume your regular savings contributions and allocate additional funds, if available, until your emergency fund is fully replenished.

Regularly Review and Adjust: As your financial situation evolves, regularly review your emergency fund and make adjustments as needed. Reassess your savings goal, considering changes in income, expenses, or personal circumstances. Adjust your contributions accordingly to ensure your emergency fund remains aligned with your current needs.

Celebrate Milestones: Building an emergency fund is a significant accomplishment. Celebrate milestones along the way to stay motivated and reinforce positive financial habits. Whether it's reaching a certain savings threshold or successfully handling an unexpected expense without relying on debt, acknowledge your progress and use it as fuel to continue building your financial resilience

Chapter 9: Investing in the Stock Market: Unleashing the Power of Wealth Creation

The stock market offers a world of opportunities for wealth creation and long-term financial growth. In this chapter, we will delve into the fundamentals of investing in the stock market, explore different investment strategies, and provide insights into making informed investment decisions.

Section 1: Understanding the Stock Market

1.1 What is the Stock Market?: Gain a clear understanding of what the stock market is and how it functions. Learn about stocks, shares, and the role of stock exchanges in facilitating the buying and selling of securities.

1.2 Benefits and Risks of Stock Market Investing: Explore the potential benefits of investing in stocks, including capital appreciation and dividend income. Understand the inherent risks associated with stock market investments and learn strategies to mitigate those risks.

Section 2: Getting Started with Stock Market Investing

2.1 Setting Investment Goals: Define your investment goals based on your financial aspirations, time horizon, and risk tolerance. Whether it's building long-term wealth, saving for retirement, or funding a specific financial goal, align your investment strategy with your objectives.

2.2 Establishing an Investment Budget: Determine the amount of money you are willing to invest in the stock market. Create an investment budget that takes into account your financial situation, expenses, and other financial obligations.

2.3 Building a Diversified Portfolio: Learn the importance of diversification and how to construct a well-balanced investment portfolio. Explore different asset classes, such as stocks, bonds, and mutual funds, to spread risk and maximize potential returns.

Section 3: Investment Strategies

3.1 Fundamental Analysis: Dive into the world of fundamental analysis, which involves assessing a company's financial health, competitive advantage, and growth prospects. Learn how to analyze financial statements, evaluate key financial ratios, and make informed investment decisions based on a company's fundamentals.

3.2 Technical Analysis: Discover the principles of technical analysis, which involves studying stock price patterns, trends, and market indicators. Explore charting techniques and tools to identify potential buying and selling opportunities in the stock market.

3.3 Value Investing: Uncover the principles of value investing, popularized by legendary investor Warren Buffett. Learn how to identify undervalued stocks with solid fundamentals and long-term growth potential.

3.4 Growth Investing: Explore the concept of growth investing, focusing on companies with high growth rates and the potential for significant capital appreciation. Understand the key factors to consider when evaluating growth stocks and building a growth-oriented investment strategy.

Section 4: Risk Management and Portfolio Monitoring

4.1 Risk Management Strategies: Develop risk management strategies to protect your investment portfolio. Learn about concepts such as stop-loss orders, diversification, and asset allocation to minimize potential losses and preserve capital.

4.2 Portfolio Monitoring and Rebalancing: Understand the importance of regularly monitoring your investment portfolio. Learn how to review and rebalance your holdings to maintain your desired asset allocation and adapt to changing market conditions.

Section 5: Common Stock Market Pitfalls and How to Avoid Them

5.1 Emotional Investing: Explore the impact of emotions on investment decisions and learn strategies to overcome common behavioral biases. Develop a disciplined approach to investing based on research, analysis, and a long-term perspective.

5.2 Timing the Market: Understand the futility of market timing and the potential risks associated with trying to predict short-term market movements. Embrace a long-term investment strategy that focuses on the fundamentals and avoids the pitfalls of market timing.

5.3 Investor Education and Continued Learning: Emphasize the importance of ongoing investor education and continuous learning. Stay informed about market trends, industry developments, and financial news to make well-informed investment decisions.

Section 1: Understanding the Stock Market

1.1 What is the Stock Market?

The stock market is a dynamic marketplace where investors buy and sell securities, primarily stocks and shares, representing ownership in publicly traded companies. It serves as a platform for companies to raise capital by issuing stocks to investors, and for investors to trade these stocks among themselves.

Within the stock market, various stock exchanges operate, such as the New York Stock Exchange (NYSE), Nasdaq, London Stock Exchange (LSE), and Tokyo Stock Exchange (TSE). These exchanges provide the infrastructure and regulations necessary for smooth trading and ensure transparency in the marketplace.

1.2 Benefits of Stock Market Investing

Investing in the stock market offers several benefits:

1.2.1 Potential for Capital Appreciation: One of the primary attractions of the stock market is the potential for capital appreciation. As companies grow and become more profitable, the value of their stocks can increase, allowing investors to earn a profit when they sell their shares.

1.2.2 Dividend Income: Many established companies distribute a portion of their profits as dividends to shareholders. By investing in dividend-paying stocks, investors can earn regular income on their investments.

1.2.3 Ownership and Influence: Owning shares of a company gives investors a stake in the company's ownership. Depending on the number of shares held, investors may have the right to vote on certain corporate matters, such as the appointment of board members.

1.2.4 Portfolio Diversification: Investing in stocks allows for diversification within an investment portfolio. By spreading investments across different industries and companies, investors can reduce their exposure to individual stock risks and increase the potential for long-term returns.

1.2.5 Liquidity: The stock market provides liquidity, meaning investors can easily buy or sell stocks at prevailing market prices. This liquidity allows investors to convert their investments into cash relatively quickly if needed.

1.3 Risks of Stock Market Investing

While stock market investing offers potential rewards, it is important to understand and manage the associated risks:

1.3.1 Volatility: Stock prices can be highly volatile, influenced by various factors such as economic conditions, company performance, industry trends, and investor sentiment. Fluctuations in stock prices can result in potential gains or losses.

1.3.2 Market Risk: The overall market conditions, including factors like interest rates, inflation, and geopolitical events, can impact stock prices. Economic downturns or market crashes can lead to significant declines in stock values.

1.3.3 Company-Specific Risk: Investing in individual stocks carries the risk of company-specific events, such as poor financial performance, management issues, or legal challenges. These events can negatively impact the value of the stock.

1.3.4 Liquidity Risk: In certain market conditions, it may be challenging to find buyers or sellers for specific stocks, potentially leading to limited liquidity. Illiquid stocks can make it difficult to enter or exit positions at desired prices.

1.3.5 Information and Market Efficiency: The stock market is influenced by the availability and dissemination of information. Investors need to consider the efficiency of the market in quickly reflecting new information in stock prices.

In the next sections, we will explore how to get started with stock market investing, set investment goals, and build a diversified portfolio that aligns with your financial objectives and risk tolerance. By understanding the benefits and risks of stock market investing, you can make informed decisions to maximize your investment potential.

Section 2: Getting Started with Stock Market Investing

2.1 Setting Investment Goals

Before diving into stock market investing, it is crucial to define your investment goals. Setting clear and realistic goals will guide your investment strategy and help you stay focused on your financial objectives. Consider the following steps when setting investment goals:

2.1.1 Assess Your Financial Situation: Start by evaluating your current financial situation, including your income, expenses, savings, and any outstanding debts. Understanding your financial standing will provide a realistic context for setting investment goals.

2.1.2 Define Your Time Horizon: Determine the time frame for achieving your investment goals. Are you investing for short-term objectives, such as purchasing a car or going on a vacation? Or are you focused on long-term goals like retirement planning? Clarify your time horizon to align your investment strategy accordingly.

2.1.3 Consider Risk Tolerance: Assess your risk tolerance, which refers to your comfort level with potential investment volatility and fluctuations. Are you willing to take on higher risks for potentially higher returns, or do you prefer a more conservative approach? Understanding your risk tolerance will help shape your investment decisions.

2.1.4 Establish Specific Goals: Define specific investment goals that are measurable and attainable. For example, your goal might be to save a certain amount for a down payment on a house or to accumulate a specific retirement fund. Quantify your goals to provide a clear target to work towards.

2.1.5 Prioritize Your Goals: If you have multiple investment goals, prioritize them based on importance and urgency. Determine which goals are short-term, medium-term, and long-term to create a timeline for achieving each one.

2.1.6 Review and Adjust: Regularly review and reassess your investment goals. As your financial situation and priorities evolve, you may need to modify or update your goals accordingly. Flexibility and adaptability are key in ensuring your investment strategy remains aligned with your changing circumstances.

2.2 Creating an Investment Budget

Once you have established your investment goals, it's essential to create an investment budget. An investment budget outlines the amount of money you are willing to allocate towards your investment activities. Follow these steps to create an effective investment budget:

2.2.1 Evaluate Your Cash Flow: Analyze your income and expenses to understand your cash flow. Identify surplus funds that can be allocated towards investments. If you have limited disposable income, consider ways to increase your savings or reduce unnecessary expenses to free up funds for investing.

2.2.2 Determine Your Investment Amount: Decide how much money you are comfortable investing. Consider your risk tolerance and the time horizon of your investment goals when determining the investment amount.

2.2.3 Consider Regular Contributions: To build wealth steadily, consider making regular contributions to your investment portfolio. Setting up automatic contributions from your income can ensure consistent investing and take advantage of dollar-cost averaging, which helps average out the purchase price of investments over time.

2.2.4 Account for Other Financial Obligations: While investing is important, it's essential to prioritize other financial obligations, such as debt repayment and emergency savings. Ensure that your investment budget allows for these obligations while still allowing room for growth in your investment portfolio.

2.2.5 Seek Professional Advice if Needed: If you are unsure about creating an investment budget or need guidance in managing your finances, consider seeking advice from a financial advisor. They can provide personalized recommendations based on your specific financial situation and goals.

By setting investment goals and creating an investment budget, you lay the foundation for a structured and purposeful approach to stock market investing. These steps will help you stay focused, make informed decisions, and work towards achieving your financial aspirations. In the next section, we will explore the concept of portfolio diversification to manage risk and maximize potential returns.

Section 3: Portfolio Diversification

Diversification is a fundamental principle of investment that aims to reduce risk by spreading investments across different asset classes, industries, and geographical regions. It is an essential strategy to manage risk and optimize potential returns in a well-rounded investment portfolio. In this section, we will explore the concept of portfolio diversification and its key considerations.

3.1 The Importance of Diversification

Diversification is important for several reasons:

3.1.1 Risk Reduction: By diversifying your portfolio, you can mitigate the impact of individual investment losses. Different assets or sectors may perform differently under various market conditions, and having a mix of investments can help offset potential losses in one area with gains in another.

3.1.2 Potential for Higher Returns: Diversification allows you to tap into different investment opportunities. While some investments may underperform, others may excel, potentially leading to overall higher returns. By spreading your investments across various assets, you increase the likelihood of capturing positive investment trends.

3.1.3 Stability and Resilience: A diversified portfolio tends to be more stable and resilient in the face of market volatility. When one asset class or sector experiences a downturn, other investments may help balance out the impact, reducing the overall portfolio volatility.

3.2 Key Considerations for Diversification

When diversifying your investment portfolio, consider the following factors:

3.2.1 Asset Allocation: Determine the appropriate allocation of your investments across different asset classes, such as stocks, bonds, real estate, commodities, and cash equivalents. The allocation should align with your investment goals, risk tolerance, and time horizon. A well-diversified portfolio typically includes a mix of asset classes to balance risk and potential returns.

3.2.2 Geographic Diversification: Investing in different regions and countries can provide exposure to various economic conditions and reduce country-specific risks. Consider diversifying your portfolio by including investments from different geographical areas.

3.2.3 Sector Diversification: Allocate your investments across different sectors or industries to avoid concentration risk. Industries can experience cycles of growth and decline, and diversifying across sectors helps protect your portfolio from the adverse impact of a downturn in a specific sector.

3.2.4 Company Size and Type: Diversify your portfolio by investing in companies of different sizes (large-cap, mid-cap, small-cap) and types (growth, value). Each category offers unique risk and return characteristics, and diversifying across these categories can enhance your portfolio's stability.

3.2.5 Investment Instruments: Explore various investment instruments within each asset class. For example, within the stock market, diversify between individual stocks, exchange-traded funds (ETFs), and mutual funds. Each instrument offers different benefits and risks, and diversification across them can provide a balanced exposure.

3.2.6 Regular Portfolio Review: Periodically review your portfolio to ensure it remains diversified and aligned with your investment goals. As market conditions change, some investments may outperform or underperform, leading to a shift in the portfolio's diversification. Rebalance your portfolio by adjusting the allocation if necessary.

3.3 Managing Diversification

While diversification is important, it's essential to strike a balance. Over-diversification can dilute potential returns and make it challenging to track and manage the portfolio effectively. Consider the following tips to manage diversification effectively:

3.3.1 Set Realistic Diversification Targets: Define your diversification targets based on your investment goals and risk tolerance. It's not necessary to own every investment available; focus on achieving an appropriate level of diversification.

3.3.2 Monitor Correlations: Understand the correlations between different investments in your portfolio. Correlation measures the relationship between the price movements of two assets. By including assets with low correlations, you can achieve better diversification benefits.

3.3.3 Stay Informed: Stay updated on market trends, economic indicators, and industry developments. This information can help you make informed decisions when diversifying your portfolio and adjusting allocations.

3.3.4 Seek Professional Guidance: If you are unsure about diversification strategies or need assistance in managing a diversified portfolio, consider consulting with a financial advisor. They can provide valuable insights and recommendations tailored to your specific investment objectives.

By incorporating diversification principles into your investment strategy, you can reduce risk, enhance potential returns, and create a resilient portfolio. Diversification is a key element of successful long-term investing, and understanding its principles will empower you to make sound investment decisions. In the next section, we will explore different investment strategies and approaches to consider for building wealth.

Section 4: Building Wealth through Long-Term Investments

Building wealth is a goal shared by many individuals, and one effective way to achieve this is through long-term investments. In this section, we will explore various strategies and considerations for building wealth over time.

4.1 The Power of Long-Term Investments

Long-term investments offer several advantages when it comes to building wealth:

4.1.1 Compounding Returns: The power of compounding is a fundamental concept in long-term investing. By reinvesting your earnings, you can generate additional returns on your initial investment, which can significantly accelerate the growth of your wealth over time.

4.1.2 Ride Out Market Volatility: Long-term investments provide the opportunity to ride out market fluctuations. While short-term market volatility can cause temporary declines in the value of investments, the market historically tends to recover over the long term, allowing patient investors to benefit from the upward trajectory.

4.1.3 Time to Weather Economic Cycles: Economic cycles are a natural part of the market. By adopting a long-term investment approach, you can give your investments sufficient time to weather these cycles. This reduces the impact of short-term market fluctuations and increases the likelihood of achieving positive returns over an extended period.

4.2 Considerations for Long-Term Investments

When embarking on a journey to build wealth through long-term investments, it's important to consider the following factors:

4.2.1 Investment Objectives: Clearly define your investment objectives, whether it's retirement planning, funding a child's education, or achieving financial independence. Having specific goals will guide your investment strategy and help you stay focused on the long term.

4.2.2 Risk Tolerance: Understand your risk tolerance and align it with your investment approach. Long-term investments may involve market fluctuations and potential losses in the short term. Assess your comfort level with risk and determine the level of volatility you are willing to tolerate in pursuit of long-term growth.

4.2.3 Asset Allocation: Develop a well-diversified asset allocation strategy based on your risk profile and investment goals. Allocate your investments across different asset classes such as stocks, bonds, real estate, and cash equivalents to spread risk and capture growth opportunities.

4.2.4 Regular Contributions: Consider making regular contributions to your investment portfolio. Systematic investing, such as monthly contributions, allows you to take advantage of dollar-cost averaging, where you buy more shares when prices are low and fewer shares when prices are high. This strategy can potentially enhance long-term returns.

4.2.5 Patience and Discipline: Building wealth through long-term investments requires patience and discipline. Stay focused on your investment strategy and resist the temptation to make impulsive decisions based on short-term market fluctuations. Stick to your long-term plan and avoid reactionary behavior.

4.3 Investment Vehicles for Long-Term Growth

Several investment vehicles are well-suited for long-term wealth building:

4.3.1 Stock Market: Investing in individual stocks or diversified stock market indices can offer substantial long-term growth potential. Research companies, assess their fundamentals, and select investments that align with your investment strategy.

4.3.2 Mutual Funds and Exchange-Traded Funds (ETFs): These investment vehicles pool funds from multiple investors to invest in a diversified portfolio of stocks, bonds, or other assets. Mutual funds and ETFs provide instant diversification and professional management, making them attractive options for long-term investors.

4.3.3 Retirement Accounts: Contributing to retirement accounts, such as Individual Retirement Accounts (IRAs) or employer-sponsored 401(k) plans, offers tax advantages and long-term growth opportunities. Maximize your contributions to take full advantage of tax benefits and potential employer matches.

4.3.4 Real Estate: Investing in real estate can provide long-term appreciation and income potential. Whether through direct ownership or real estate investment trusts (REITs), real estate investments can diversify your portfolio and offer a hedge against inflation.

4.4 Evaluating and Monitoring Investments

Regularly evaluating and monitoring your long-term investments is crucial for success. Consider the following practices:

4.4.1 Review Performance: Assess the performance of your investments periodically. Compare their performance against relevant benchmarks and your investment objectives. This evaluation will help you identify areas of strength and areas that may require adjustments.

4.4.2 Rebalance Portfolio: Rebalance your portfolio periodically to maintain your desired asset allocation. As different investments grow at varying rates, your portfolio may become imbalanced. Rebalancing ensures that you realign your investments according to your intended strategy.

4.4.3 Stay Informed: Keep yourself informed about market trends, economic indicators, and changes in the investment landscape. Stay up-to-date with financial news, research reports, and industry insights to make informed decisions about your long-term investments.

4.4.4 Seek Professional Advice: If needed, seek guidance from a qualified financial advisor. They can provide personalized advice based on your financial situation, investment goals, and risk tolerance. A professional advisor can offer valuable insights and help you navigate the complexities of long-term investing.

By embracing a long-term investment mindset, considering key factors, and selecting appropriate investment vehicles, you can build wealth steadily over time. In the next chapter, we will explore specific strategies for managing your personal finances and optimizing your financial well-being.

Section 5: Managing Personal Finances for Long-Term Success

Effective management of personal finances is a critical aspect of building long-term wealth. In this section, we will discuss various strategies and practices to help you optimize your financial well-being and achieve your financial goals.

5.1 Budgeting and Expense Management

5.1.1 Create a Budget: Start by creating a comprehensive budget that outlines your income and expenses. Identify areas where you can reduce unnecessary expenses and allocate funds towards savings and investments. A budget provides a clear roadmap for managing your finances effectively.

5.1.2 Track Your Spending: Keep track of your expenses to gain insights into your spending patterns. Use financial management tools, mobile apps, or spreadsheets to record your expenditures. Regularly review your spending habits and make adjustments as needed to align with your financial goals.

5.1.3 Prioritize Savings: Make savings a priority in your budget. Aim to save a portion of your income each month, ideally at least 10-20%. Establish an emergency fund to cover unexpected expenses and save for future financial goals, such as buying a home, funding education, or retirement.

5.2 Debt Management

5.2.1 Reduce High-Interest Debt: Prioritize paying off high-interest debt, such as credit cards or personal loans. Allocate extra funds towards these debts to minimize interest payments and accelerate your debt repayment. Consider debt consolidation strategies to simplify your debt obligations and potentially lower interest rates.

5.2.2 Smart Borrowing: When taking on new debt, carefully assess the terms and conditions. Compare interest rates, fees, and repayment options from different lenders. Borrow responsibly and only when necessary, ensuring that the debt aligns with your financial goals and can be comfortably repaid.

5.3 Establishing an Emergency Fund

5.3.1 Importance of Emergency Fund: Building an emergency fund is crucial for financial stability. Aim to save at least three to six months' worth of living expenses. This fund acts as a safety net during unexpected events such as job loss, medical emergencies, or major home repairs.

5.3.2 Automate Savings: Set up automatic transfers from your income to your emergency fund. Treat it as a non-negotiable expense, just like paying bills. This ensures consistent contributions and helps you build your emergency fund gradually over time.

5.4 Investing for Long-Term Growth

5.4.1 Understand Investment Options: Educate yourself about various investment vehicles, such as stocks, bonds, mutual funds, and retirement accounts. Understand the risk-return tradeoff associated with different investment options and align them with your risk tolerance and long-term goals.

5.4.2 Start Early: Begin investing as early as possible to take advantage of the power of compounding. Even small contributions can grow significantly over time due to the compounding effect. The earlier you start, the longer your investments have to grow.

5.4.3 Diversify Your Portfolio: Diversification is key to managing risk and maximizing returns. Allocate your investments across different asset classes and industries to spread risk. Consider diversifying internationally to access global markets and broaden your investment opportunities.

5.4.4 Seek Professional Guidance: If you're unsure about investment strategies or need assistance, consider consulting with a financial advisor. They can provide personalized advice based on your financial situation and goals, helping you make informed investment decisions.

5.5 Protecting Your Financial Health

5.5.1 Insurance Coverage: Review your insurance coverage to ensure adequate protection for your assets, health, and income. Consider policies such as life insurance, health insurance, disability insurance, and property insurance. Regularly reassess your insurance needs as your circumstances evolve.

5.5.2 Estate Planning: Develop an estate plan to protect your assets and ensure the orderly distribution of your wealth. Create a will, establish trusts if necessary, and designate beneficiaries for your accounts. Seek legal advice to ensure your estate plan aligns with your intentions and legal requirements.

By implementing effective budgeting strategies, managing debt responsibly, building an emergency fund, investing for long-term growth, and protecting your financial health, you can set a solid foundation for long-term financial success. In the next chapter, we will explore various business ideas and opportunities for aspiring entrepreneurs.

Chapter 10: Exploring Business Ideas and Opportunities

Starting a business can be a fulfilling and rewarding journey, offering opportunities for financial independence and creative expression. In this chapter, we will explore various business ideas and opportunities that aspiring entrepreneurs can consider. Remember that success in entrepreneurship often requires dedication, innovation, and a willingness to adapt to changing market conditions.

Section 10.1: Home-Based Businesses

Running a business from the comfort of your own home offers flexibility and convenience. It allows you to pursue your entrepreneurial dreams while balancing personal commitments. In this section, we will explore various home-based business ideas that you can consider.

10.1.1 Freelancing and Consulting

One of the most popular home-based business options is freelancing or consulting. If you have specialized skills and expertise in areas such as graphic design, web development, marketing, writing, or business strategy, you can offer your services on a freelance basis. Many businesses and individuals are willing to pay for high-quality work on a project-by-project basis, making freelancing a viable option for generating income.

To succeed as a freelancer or consultant, build a strong portfolio that showcases your skills and previous work. Network with potential clients through online platforms, professional associations, or industry events. Leverage your expertise to provide valuable solutions and meet clients' needs effectively. Remember to communicate clearly, deliver projects on time, and provide exceptional customer service to build a positive reputation in your field.

10.1.2 Online Retail

With the rise of e-commerce, starting an online retail business has become increasingly accessible. You can create an online store and sell products through popular platforms like Amazon, eBay, or Etsy. Consider identifying a unique niche or target market to differentiate yourself from the competition.

When setting up an online retail business, conduct thorough market research to identify profitable product opportunities. Source products from reputable suppliers and ensure their quality meets customer expectations. Optimize your online store by utilizing compelling product descriptions, high-quality images, and customer reviews. Implement effective marketing strategies such as search engine optimization (SEO), social media marketing, and email campaigns to drive traffic and generate sales.

10.1.3 Virtual Assisting

Virtual assisting has gained popularity in recent years, as businesses and entrepreneurs seek remote support for various administrative tasks. As a virtual assistant, you can offer services such as administrative support, social media management, customer support, or email management.

To thrive as a virtual assistant, showcase your organizational skills, attention to detail, and ability to multitask. Establish clear communication channels with clients, utilizing tools like email, project management software, or video conferencing. Stay up to date with the latest virtual assistant tools and technologies to enhance your productivity and efficiency. Develop strong relationships with your clients by providing reliable and professional support.

Remember that building a successful home-based business requires discipline, time management, and a dedicated workspace. Set boundaries to separate your work life from your personal life, and establish a routine that allows you to focus on your business goals. Embrace continuous learning and skill development to stay competitive in the ever-evolving business landscape.

In the next section, we will explore service-based businesses that can be operated from home, providing opportunities for entrepreneurs to leverage their skills and passions effectively.

Section 10.2: Service-Based Businesses

Service-based businesses offer valuable expertise, skills, and assistance to clients in various industries. They often involve direct interaction with customers, allowing you to provide personalized services tailored to their specific needs. In this section, we will explore different service-based business ideas that you can consider.

10.2.1 Personal Training and Wellness Coaching

If you have a passion for health and fitness, starting a personal training or wellness coaching business can be a fulfilling venture. As a personal trainer or wellness coach, you can help clients achieve their fitness goals, improve their overall well-being, and adopt healthy lifestyle habits.

To establish yourself in the personal training or wellness coaching industry, consider obtaining relevant certifications or qualifications to demonstrate your expertise. Develop customized fitness or wellness plans based on individual client needs and goals. Offer one-on-one training sessions, group classes, or online coaching services to reach a wider audience. Build strong relationships with your clients by providing guidance, motivation, and ongoing support.

10.2.2 Event Planning

Event planning is a service-based business that requires excellent organizational and coordination skills. As an event planner, you will be responsible for organizing and executing various events, such as weddings, corporate gatherings, conferences, or parties.

To excel in the event planning industry, establish a network of reliable vendors and suppliers. Develop strong communication and negotiation skills to ensure smooth collaborations with clients and event stakeholders. Pay attention to detail, create memorable experiences, and exceed client expectations. Utilize event management software or tools to streamline your processes and stay organized. Marketing your services through social media, referrals, and partnerships can help attract clients and grow your business.

10.2.3 Pet Services

The pet industry continues to experience significant growth, creating opportunities for service-based businesses related to pet care. Services such as pet sitting, dog walking, grooming, or training are in high demand as pet owners seek reliable and trusted professionals to care for their furry companions.

To start a successful pet services business, build a strong reputation by providing exceptional care and services. Develop a clear pricing structure and service offerings that cater to different customer needs. Invest in proper training and certifications, especially for pet grooming or training services. Establish partnerships with local veterinarians, pet stores, or animal shelters to expand your network and gain referrals.

Remember that in service-based businesses, customer satisfaction and positive word-of-mouth are crucial for success. Focus on delivering exceptional services, building long-term relationships with clients, and continuously improving your skills and knowledge. In the next section, we will explore opportunities in technology and innovation that can lead to lucrative service-based businesses.

Section 10.3: Technology and Innovation

Technology and innovation play a significant role in shaping the modern business landscape. Leveraging advancements in technology can provide opportunities for entrepreneurs to create innovative service-based businesses. In this section, we will explore some technology-driven business ideas.

10.3.1 App Development and Mobile Solutions

The growing popularity of smartphones has created a demand for mobile applications across various industries. If you have programming skills or access to a team of developers, starting an app development business can be a lucrative venture. Identify market gaps or specific needs within industries and develop innovative apps that provide solutions.

To succeed in the app development industry, stay up to date with the latest mobile technologies and trends. Collaborate with designers, marketers, and usability experts to create user-friendly and visually appealing apps. Offer post-launch support, updates, and enhancements to ensure the continuous improvement of your apps. Promote your services through online platforms, social media, and targeted marketing campaigns.

10.3.2 Digital Marketing and Social Media Management

In today's digital age, businesses rely on effective online marketing strategies to reach their target audience and generate leads. If you have a strong understanding of digital marketing, social media platforms, and content creation, starting a digital marketing or social media management business can be a promising opportunity.

Offer services such as search engine optimization (SEO), social media marketing, content creation, email marketing, or paid advertising. Develop customized strategies tailored to each client's specific goals and target audience. Stay updated with the latest digital marketing trends, tools, and algorithms to ensure the success of your campaigns. Demonstrate the value of your services by showcasing previous results and client success stories.

10.3.3 Virtual Reality (VR) and Augmented Reality (AR) Experiences

Virtual reality (VR) and augmented reality (AR) technologies are gaining traction in various industries, including gaming, education, tourism, and real estate. If you have a background in computer graphics or programming, starting a business that specializes in VR or AR experiences can be a unique and exciting venture.

Create immersive virtual or augmented reality experiences for clients, such as virtual tours, interactive training programs, or engaging gaming experiences. Collaborate with industry-specific businesses to develop tailored VR or AR solutions. Stay abreast of the latest advancements in VR and AR technologies to offer cutting-edge experiences to your clients. Market your services to businesses, educational institutions, or organizations seeking innovative and engaging solutions.

When starting a technology-driven service-based business, focus on delivering exceptional quality, staying ahead of the curve with technological advancements, and providing outstanding customer support. Leverage your expertise to offer unique and valuable solutions that meet the evolving needs of your target market. In the next section, we will explore opportunities in the realm of franchises and proven business models

Section 10.4: Franchising and Proven Business Models

Franchising offers a way to enter the business world with an established brand and a proven business model. By partnering with a reputable franchise, you can leverage their success, support, and systems to start your own business. In this section, we will explore the potential of franchising and some popular franchise opportunities.

10.4.1 Fast Food and Quick-Service Restaurants

Fast food and quick-service restaurants are some of the most recognizable and successful franchise models globally. Brands like McDonald's, Subway, or Domino's Pizza have established a strong presence and loyal customer base. Investing in a fast food or quick-service restaurant franchise can provide a turnkey solution for aspiring entrepreneurs.

Franchise opportunities in the food industry offer training, operational support, marketing assistance, and a well-established supply chain. Ensure you thoroughly research the franchisor, evaluate the financials, and understand the terms and obligations before making a commitment. Consider factors such as location, target market, competition, and local demand when choosing a specific franchise opportunity.

10.4.2 Fitness Centers and Gyms

The fitness industry continues to grow, with an increasing focus on health and wellness. Fitness centers and gyms offer franchise opportunities that cater to the growing demand for fitness services. Brands like Anytime Fitness, Planet Fitness, or Orangetheory Fitness have successfully expanded through franchising.

When considering a fitness franchise, evaluate the brand's reputation, target market, competitive advantage, and support provided by the franchisor. Location plays a crucial role in the success of a fitness center, so choose a suitable area with a potential customer base. Understand the financial aspects, including franchise fees, royalties, and equipment costs, to make an informed decision.

10.4.3 Home Services and Maintenance

Home services and maintenance franchises provide essential services for homeowners, such as cleaning, landscaping, plumbing, or pest control. These businesses capitalize on the demand for professional services that save homeowners time and effort.

Research reputable home services franchises that align with your skills and interests. Consider factors like initial investment, ongoing support, marketing strategies, and the potential for scalability. Ensure you have a thorough understanding of the local market, competition, and customer preferences in your target area.

10.4.4 Senior Care and Assisted Living

With an aging population, senior care and assisted living franchises have experienced significant growth. These franchises offer services such as in-home care, senior companion services, or assisted living facilities.

When exploring senior care franchises, research the industry's regulations, training requirements, and certifications. Understand the specific services provided, such as personal care, medication management, or specialized care for individuals with Alzheimer's or dementia. Consider the demographic and market demand in your area, as well as the competition and potential for growth.

Franchising provides an opportunity to enter the business world with a proven concept, established brand recognition, and ongoing support. However, it is essential to conduct thorough due diligence, review the franchisor's disclosure documents, and seek professional advice before committing to a franchise opportunity. In the next section, we will explore the realm of e-commerce and online business ideas.

Section 10.5: E-commerce and Online Business Ideas

The rise of the internet and e-commerce has opened up a world of opportunities for entrepreneurs to start and grow online businesses. In this section, we will explore various e-commerce and online business ideas that you can pursue.

10.5.1 Dropshipping

Dropshipping is a popular business model that allows you to sell products online without holding inventory. With dropshipping, you partner with suppliers who handle the fulfillment and shipment of products directly to your customers. This eliminates the need for warehousing and inventory management.

To start a dropshipping business, identify a niche or product category that you want to focus on. Research and select reliable suppliers who offer quality products and efficient shipping services. Build an e-commerce website or utilize existing online marketplaces to showcase your products and attract customers. Implement effective marketing strategies to drive traffic to your store and optimize conversions.

10.5.2 Print-on-Demand Merchandise

Print-on-demand (POD) allows you to create and sell custom-designed merchandise without upfront inventory costs. With POD, products such as t-shirts, hoodies, mugs, or phone cases are produced and shipped on-demand as customers place orders.

To start a print-on-demand business, you need to create unique designs or collaborate with talented designers. Partner with POD platforms or printers that offer a wide range of customizable products. Set up an online store or integrate your products with popular e-commerce platforms. Focus on building a brand, marketing your products through social media, influencer collaborations, and targeted advertising.

10.5.3 Online Consulting and Coaching

If you have expertise in a specific field or industry, starting an online consulting or coaching business can be a rewarding venture. Whether it's business consulting, career coaching, life coaching, or specialized advice, many individuals and businesses are seeking guidance and mentorship.

To establish an online consulting or coaching business, define your niche and target audience. Build a professional website or create an online platform to showcase your services, credentials, and testimonials. Develop compelling content, such as blog posts, videos, or webinars, to demonstrate your knowledge and attract potential clients. Leverage social media, professional networks, and partnerships to expand your reach and establish yourself as an authority in your field.

10.5.4 Affiliate Marketing

Affiliate marketing allows you to earn commissions by promoting other people's products or services. As an affiliate marketer, you recommend products through your website, blog, social media, or email marketing campaigns. When someone makes a purchase through your referral link, you earn a commission.

To start an affiliate marketing business, identify a niche or industry you are passionate about and select relevant products or services to promote. Build an online platform, such as a blog or website, where you can create valuable content and product reviews. Join affiliate networks or programs that offer a wide range of products and competitive commission rates. Implement effective marketing strategies to drive traffic and conversions.

E-commerce and online business ideas provide flexibility, scalability, and global reach. However, it is crucial to conduct market research, develop a solid business plan, and continually adapt to the evolving digital landscape. In the next section, we will explore the world of real estate and property investment opportunities.

Chapter 11: Real Estate and Property Investment

Real estate has long been considered a reliable and lucrative investment opportunity. In this chapter, we will delve into the world of real estate and explore various strategies and considerations for property investment.

11.1 Understanding Real Estate Investment

Before diving into real estate investment, it's essential to have a clear understanding of the basics. This section will provide an overview of real estate investment, including different property types, financing options, and potential risks and rewards.

11.1.1 Property Types

Real estate offers a diverse range of property types to invest in. These include residential properties (such as single-family homes, condos, or apartment buildings), commercial properties (such as office spaces, retail properties, or industrial buildings), and specialized properties (such as hotels, warehouses, or healthcare facilities). Understanding the different property types and their dynamics will help you identify the most suitable investment opportunities for your goals.

11.1.2 Financing Options

Financing plays a crucial role in real estate investment. This section will explore various financing options available to investors, such as traditional mortgages, private loans, seller financing, or partnerships. Understanding the pros and cons of each option and assessing your financial situation will help you make informed decisions when acquiring investment properties.

11.1.3 Risks and Rewards

Like any investment, real estate carries its own set of risks and rewards. This section will discuss the potential risks associated with real estate investment, such as market fluctuations, vacancies, or unforeseen expenses. It will also highlight the rewards, including rental income, property appreciation, tax benefits, and portfolio diversification. Understanding the risk-reward balance is crucial for managing expectations and making sound investment choices.

11.2 Rental Property Investment

Rental properties are a popular choice among real estate investors, providing a steady stream of income and long-term wealth accumulation. This section will explore the key considerations and strategies for successful rental property investment.

11.2.1 Market Analysis

Before investing in rental properties, conducting thorough market analysis is crucial. This includes assessing the local rental market, vacancy rates, rental demand, and potential rental income. Analyzing market trends, demographics, and economic factors will help you identify areas with strong rental potential and favorable investment conditions.

11.2.2 Property Selection

Choosing the right rental property is essential for long-term success. This section will discuss factors to consider when selecting rental properties, including location, property condition, rental potential, and target tenant market. It will also explore strategies for identifying undervalued properties or properties with value-add potential.

11.2.3 Rental Property Management

Efficient property management is key to maximizing rental property investment returns. This section will delve into property management considerations, including tenant screening, lease agreements, maintenance and repairs, rent collection, and legal compliance. It will highlight the importance of proactive management practices and building positive landlord-tenant relationships.

11.3 Real Estate Investment Strategies

Beyond rental properties, there are various real estate investment strategies that can help diversify your portfolio and maximize returns. This section will explore some of these strategies, including:

11.3.1 Flipping Properties

Property flipping involves purchasing distressed properties, renovating them, and selling them for a profit. This section will discuss the essential elements of successful property flipping, including identifying potential opportunities, analyzing renovation costs, and understanding market dynamics.

11.3.2 Real Estate Investment Trusts (REITs)

REITs are investment vehicles that allow individuals to invest in real estate portfolios without direct property ownership. This section will explain the concept of REITs, their advantages, and the various types available. It will also discuss the potential risks and rewards associated with investing in REITs.

11.3.3 Real Estate Syndication

Real estate syndication involves pooling resources from multiple investors to acquire large-scale properties or projects. This section will explore the concept of real estate syndication, the roles of syndicators and investors, and the potential benefits and considerations of participating in syndicated real estate deals.

11.4 Building a Real Estate Investment Portfolio

This section will provide guidance on building a diversified real estate investment portfolio. It will discuss portfolio allocation, risk management strategies, and the importance of ongoing market analysis and evaluation. Additionally, it will explore methods for tracking performance, measuring returns, and adjusting investment strategies as needed.

Real estate investment offers a wealth of opportunities, but it requires careful planning, analysis, and execution. Whether you choose rental properties, property flipping, REITs, or syndication, understanding the fundamentals and employing smart investment strategies will increase your chances of success. In the next chapter, we will explore the world of entrepreneurship and starting your own business.

Section 11.1: Understanding Real Estate Investment

In the world of investing, real estate has always held a prominent position as a tangible and potentially lucrative asset class. Understanding the fundamentals of real estate investment is crucial for anyone looking to venture into this exciting realm. In this section, we will explore the key aspects of real estate investment, including different property types, financing options, and potential risks and rewards.

11.1.1 Property Types

Real estate encompasses a wide range of property types, each with its unique characteristics and investment potential. Residential properties, such as single-family homes, townhouses, and condominiums, offer opportunities for long-term rental income or capital appreciation. Commercial properties, including office buildings, retail spaces, and industrial warehouses, cater to businesses and can provide stable rental income. Specialized properties like hotels, healthcare facilities, or mixed-use developments offer niche investment avenues.

By understanding the nuances of each property type, investors can tailor their investment strategies to suit their goals and risk tolerance. Factors such as location, market demand, and potential for growth should be carefully considered when selecting a property type for investment.

11.1.2 Financing Options

Investing in real estate often requires substantial capital, and understanding the financing options available is essential. Traditional mortgage loans provided by banks and lending institutions are commonly used for residential and commercial property acquisitions. These loans typically involve a down payment and regular mortgage payments over an extended period.

Alternative financing options include private loans, which involve borrowing from individuals or private lenders, and seller financing, where the property seller acts as the lender. These options can provide flexibility and alternative terms compared to traditional mortgages. Additionally, partnerships and joint ventures allow investors to pool resources and share the financial burden of real estate investments.

Investors should evaluate their financial situation, creditworthiness, and investment goals to determine the most suitable financing option for their real estate endeavors.

11.1.3 Risks and Rewards

Like any investment, real estate carries inherent risks and rewards. Understanding these dynamics is vital for making informed investment decisions. Real estate investments can provide steady cash flow through rental income, potential appreciation in property value over time, and tax advantages such as depreciation deductions.

However, there are risks to consider. Market fluctuations can affect property values, and economic downturns can impact rental demand. Vacancies, maintenance costs, and unforeseen expenses are factors that can affect investment returns. It is essential to conduct thorough market research, assess potential risks, and implement risk management strategies to mitigate these challenges.

Successful real estate investors balance risk and reward by carefully selecting properties, analyzing market trends, and employing sound investment strategies.

By gaining a solid understanding of property types, financing options, and risks and rewards, aspiring real estate investors can lay a strong foundation for their investment journey. In the subsequent sections, we will explore specific strategies, such as rental property investment, property management, and alternative avenues within real estate investing.

Section 11.2: Rental Property Investment

Investing in rental properties can be a lucrative strategy for generating passive income and building long-term wealth. In this section, we will delve into the world of rental property investment, covering key considerations, strategies for property selection, and effective property management techniques.

11.2.1 Identifying Rental Property Opportunities

When seeking rental property investment opportunities, it is crucial to consider factors such as location, market demand, and property condition. Identifying neighborhoods with high rental demand, low vacancy rates, and potential for growth is essential. Analyzing rental market trends, demographics, and economic indicators can help investors make informed decisions.

Additionally, evaluating the condition of the property is crucial. Conducting thorough inspections, assessing the property's structural integrity, and estimating renovation or repair costs are necessary steps. Investors should also consider factors such as proximity to amenities, schools, transportation, and employment centers, as these can influence the property's appeal to potential tenants.

11.2.2 Financing Rental Property Investments

Financing rental property investments can be achieved through various methods. Traditional mortgage loans, similar to those used for residential properties, are commonly utilized. Investors can approach banks or lending institutions to secure favorable loan terms based on their financial situation and creditworthiness.

Alternative financing options include private lenders, crowdfunding platforms, and creative strategies such as seller financing or lease-to-own arrangements. Each financing option has its advantages and considerations, and investors should carefully evaluate the terms and implications before making a decision.

11.2.3 Property Management and Tenant Selection

Effectively managing rental properties is crucial for maximizing returns and maintaining tenant satisfaction. This involves tasks such as advertising and marketing the property, conducting tenant screenings, drafting leases, and handling maintenance and repairs.

Tenant selection is a critical aspect of property management. Conducting thorough background checks, verifying income and employment, and assessing prior rental history can help identify reliable and responsible tenants. Building positive landlord-tenant relationships, addressing maintenance requests promptly, and enforcing lease agreements are key elements of successful property management.

Moreover, implementing effective property management systems, such as rent collection processes, lease renewal strategies, and regular property inspections, can streamline operations and ensure the property remains well-maintained and profitable.

11.2.4 Cash Flow Analysis and Investment Returns

Analyzing cash flow is a fundamental aspect of rental property investment. Investors must assess potential rental income, operating expenses, and factors such as property taxes, insurance, and property management fees. Conducting thorough cash flow analysis helps determine the property's profitability and estimate investment returns.

Calculating metrics such as cash-on-cash return, cap rate, and return on investment (ROI) provides insights into the property's performance and allows investors to compare different investment opportunities. Regularly reviewing and adjusting rental rates, optimizing expenses, and continuously monitoring the rental market can help improve cash flow and overall investment returns.

Rental property investment offers the potential for consistent income, long-term appreciation, and tax benefits. By carefully considering property selection, implementing effective property management practices, and conducting thorough financial analysis, investors can build a successful rental property portfolio. In the following sections, we will explore additional investment strategies and alternative avenues within the realm of real estate investment.

Section 11.3: Alternative Avenues in Real Estate Investment

While rental properties are a popular investment option, there are alternative avenues within real estate that offer unique opportunities for wealth creation. In this section, we will explore some of these alternative investment strategies and discuss their potential benefits and considerations.

11.3.1 Real Estate Investment Trusts (REITs)

Real Estate Investment Trusts, or REITs, provide a way for individuals to invest in a diversified portfolio of income-generating real estate assets without directly owning or managing properties. REITs are companies that own, operate, or finance income-generating real estate, such as commercial properties, apartment complexes, or shopping centers.

Investing in REITs offers several advantages. Firstly, they provide an opportunity for passive real estate investment, allowing investors to benefit from rental income and property appreciation without the hassle of property management. Additionally, REITs are typically publicly traded on stock exchanges, offering liquidity and ease of buying and selling compared to direct property ownership. They also provide the potential for dividend income, as REITs are required to distribute a significant portion of their earnings to shareholders.

However, investors should consider factors such as management fees, market risks, and the performance track record of the REIT before investing. Conducting thorough research, analyzing the REIT's portfolio composition and financials, and understanding the specific risks associated with the real estate sectors in which the REIT operates is crucial.

11.3.2 Real Estate Crowdfunding

Real estate crowdfunding platforms have emerged as an alternative way for investors to participate in real estate projects with smaller capital contributions. Crowdfunding platforms connect investors with real estate developers or operators seeking capital for their projects.

Investing in real estate crowdfunding offers several advantages. It allows for diversification by participating in multiple projects with varying risk profiles and investment terms. Crowdfunding platforms also provide access to investment opportunities that were previously available only to institutional investors. Moreover, investors can choose projects based on their preferences, such as residential, commercial, or specialized properties.

However, investors should carefully evaluate the credibility and track record of the crowdfunding platform and the projects they offer. Thoroughly reviewing the project details, including the business plan, financial projections, and risk factors, is essential. Investors should also consider the platform's fees, investment structure, and the potential illiquidity of their investment until the project's completion.

11.3.3 Real Estate Partnerships and Joint Ventures

Real estate partnerships and joint ventures involve pooling resources and expertise to invest in properties or development projects. These arrangements allow investors to combine their capital, knowledge, and skills, thus expanding their investment capacity and sharing the risks and rewards.

Partnerships and joint ventures offer the benefits of shared responsibilities, access to a wider range of investment opportunities, and the ability to leverage each partner's expertise. They also provide an opportunity to learn from experienced partners and benefit from their network and industry connections.

However, it is crucial to establish clear partnership agreements that outline each partner's roles, responsibilities, and profit-sharing arrangements. Conducting due diligence on potential partners, assessing their track record, and aligning investment goals and strategies are essential for building successful real estate partnerships.

11.3.4 Real Estate Development and Property Flipping

Real estate development and property flipping involve acquiring properties, improving or renovating them, and selling them for a profit. This strategy requires a deep understanding of market dynamics, property valuations, construction processes, and local regulations.

While real estate development and property flipping can offer substantial returns, they also involve higher risks and require significant capital, expertise, and market knowledge. Investors should conduct thorough market research, evaluate the cost of renovations or construction, and carefully assess the potential market demand and resale values before undertaking such projects.

Successful development and property flipping require meticulous planning, effective project management, and the ability to adapt to market conditions. Working with experienced professionals, such as architects, contractors, and real estate agents, can enhance the chances of a profitable outcome.

Section 11.4: Investing in Stocks and Bonds

In addition to real estate, investing in stocks and bonds offers another avenue for building wealth and diversifying one's investment portfolio. Stocks represent ownership shares in publicly traded companies, while bonds are debt securities issued by corporations, governments, or municipalities.

11.4.1 Investing in Stocks

Investing in stocks allows individuals to become partial owners of companies and participate in their growth and profitability. Stocks offer the potential for capital appreciation and dividend income. Here are some key considerations when investing in stocks:

Research and Analysis: Before investing in stocks, it's essential to research and analyze the companies in which you plan to invest. This includes examining their financial statements, management team, competitive position, industry trends, and growth prospects.

Diversification: Spreading investments across different stocks and industries can help mitigate risks. Diversification allows you to capture potential gains from various sectors while reducing the impact of any single stock's performance.

Risk and Volatility: Stocks can be subject to market volatility and fluctuations. It's important to understand and evaluate the risk associated with each investment and consider your risk tolerance and investment goals.

Long-Term Perspective: Stock investing is typically more suitable for long-term goals, as the market can experience short-term fluctuations. Having a long-term perspective allows you to ride out market cycles and benefit from the compounding growth of your investments.

Monitoring and Rebalancing: Regularly monitoring your stock investments and rebalancing your portfolio can help ensure it aligns with your investment strategy. This may involve selling stocks that have reached their target price or reallocating investments to maintain a desired asset allocation.

11.4.2 Investing in Bonds

Bonds are debt instruments issued by corporations, governments, or municipalities to raise capital. Investing in bonds can provide a steady stream of income and help diversify investment portfolios. Here are key considerations when investing in bonds:

Types of Bonds: Bonds come in various forms, including government bonds, corporate bonds, municipal bonds, and treasury bonds. Each type carries different risks and yields. Understanding the characteristics and risks associated with each bond type is crucial.

Credit Ratings: Bonds are assigned credit ratings that indicate the issuer's ability to repay the debt. Higher-rated bonds generally offer lower yields but are considered less risky. Lower-rated bonds may provide higher yields but carry a higher risk of default.

Bond Maturity: Bonds have specific maturity dates, at which the principal amount is repaid. Short-term bonds typically offer lower yields but greater liquidity, while long-term bonds may provide higher yields but are subject to interest rate risk.

Interest Rates and Inflation: Interest rates and inflation can impact bond prices and yields. When interest rates rise, bond prices tend to fall, while falling interest rates can increase bond prices. Considering the prevailing interest rate environment is important when investing in bonds.

Bond Laddering: Bond laddering involves spreading investments across bonds with staggered maturity dates. This strategy helps manage interest rate risk and provides a steady income stream as bonds mature and are reinvested.

Chapter 12: Entrepreneurship and Business Ventures

Entrepreneurship is the art of identifying opportunities, taking calculated risks, and creating value through innovative business ventures. In this chapter, we will explore the world of entrepreneurship and discuss strategies for starting and growing successful businesses.

12.1 The Entrepreneurial Mindset

The entrepreneurial mindset is the foundation upon which successful businesses are built. It encompasses a unique set of attitudes, beliefs, and qualities that drive entrepreneurs to pursue their dreams and overcome obstacles. In this section, we will explore the key components of the entrepreneurial mindset and how they contribute to business success.

Vision and Passion: Entrepreneurs possess a clear vision of what they want to achieve and are fueled by a deep passion for their ideas. They have a burning desire to make a difference and create something meaningful. This vision and passion provide the drive and motivation needed to navigate the challenges that come with starting and running a business.

Risk-Taking: Entrepreneurs understand that taking calculated risks is an inherent part of the entrepreneurial journey. They embrace uncertainty and are willing to step out of their comfort zones to pursue their goals. Rather than being paralyzed by fear of failure, they see risks as opportunities for growth and learning.

Adaptability and Resilience: The business landscape is dynamic and ever-changing. Entrepreneurs must be adaptable and resilient in the face of challenges and setbacks. They understand that obstacles are part of the process and use them as stepping stones to further refine their strategies and approaches.

Creative Problem-Solving: Entrepreneurs possess a natural inclination for creative problem-solving. They approach problems from different angles, think outside the box, and are not afraid to challenge the status quo. They see problems as opportunities for innovation and view setbacks as temporary roadblocks that can be overcome with creative solutions.

Continuous Learning: Successful entrepreneurs have a thirst for knowledge and are committed to lifelong learning. They understand the importance of staying updated with industry trends, market dynamics, and technological advancements. They actively seek out opportunities to expand their knowledge and skillsets through reading, attending seminars, networking, and seeking mentorship.

Self-Discipline and Persistence: Entrepreneurship requires discipline and persistence. Entrepreneurs have the ability to stay focused on their goals, even when faced with distractions or setbacks. They possess a strong work ethic and are willing to put in the necessary time and effort to make their ventures successful.

They understand that success rarely comes overnight and are prepared to endure the ups and downs along the way.

Strong Communication and Leadership Skills: Entrepreneurs excel in communication and leadership. They possess the ability to articulate their vision, inspire others, and build strong relationships with team members, customers, investors, and other stakeholders. Effective communication and leadership are crucial for creating a cohesive and motivated team, securing partnerships, and attracting customers and investors.

Embracing Failure as a Learning Opportunity: Entrepreneurs understand that failure is not the end but rather a stepping stone to success. They embrace failures as valuable learning experiences that provide insights and lessons for future endeavors. Instead of dwelling on past mistakes, they analyze and learn from them, making adjustments to their strategies and approaches.

By cultivating and embodying the entrepreneurial mindset, aspiring entrepreneurs can set themselves on a path towards success. It is a mindset that enables individuals to see opportunities where others see challenges, take calculated risks, and persevere through obstacles. Embrace the entrepreneurial mindset, and you will unlock your full potential to create and build a successful business venture.

12.2 Strategic Planning and Goal Setting

Strategic planning and goal setting are essential components of building a successful business and achieving long-term growth and profitability. In this section, we will explore the importance of strategic planning and provide practical guidance on setting effective goals for your business.

Vision and Mission: A clear vision and mission statement lay the foundation for strategic planning. Your vision defines where you want your business to be in the future, while your mission statement outlines the purpose and values that guide your business. These statements serve as a compass, providing direction and focus for your strategic planning efforts.

SWOT Analysis: Conducting a SWOT (Strengths, Weaknesses, Opportunities, Threats) analysis helps you understand your business's internal strengths and weaknesses, as well as external opportunities and threats. By analyzing these factors, you can identify areas of competitive advantage, potential areas for improvement, and market opportunities that align with your business goals.

Market Research: Thorough market research is crucial for understanding your target market, customer needs, and industry trends. It provides insights into market size, competition, consumer preferences, and emerging opportunities. Market research enables you to make informed decisions, develop effective marketing strategies, and tailor your products or services to meet customer demands.

Setting SMART Goals: Setting goals that are Specific, Measurable, Achievable, Relevant, and Time-bound (SMART) is essential for strategic planning. SMART goals provide clarity and direction, allowing you to track progress and make necessary adjustments along the way. Each goal should be well-defined, measurable, realistic, and have a specific deadline.

Action Planning: Once you have set your goals, develop action plans that outline the specific steps and resources required to achieve them. Break down each goal into smaller, manageable tasks and assign responsibilities to team members. Establish timelines and checkpoints to monitor progress and ensure accountability.

Performance Measurement: Regularly monitor and measure your progress towards achieving your goals. Use key performance indicators (KPIs) to track important metrics, such as revenue growth, customer acquisition, customer retention, profitability, and market share. Regularly reviewing and analyzing these metrics enables you to identify areas of improvement and make data-driven decisions.

Flexibility and Adaptability: Strategic planning is not a rigid process. It requires flexibility and adaptability to respond to changing market dynamics and unforeseen circumstances. Be prepared to adjust your strategies and goals as needed, based on new information, market shifts, or internal changes. Regularly evaluate your strategic plan and make necessary refinements to ensure its relevance and effectiveness.

Communication and Alignment: Effective communication is vital for strategic planning and goal setting. Ensure that your goals, strategies, and action plans are clearly communicated to all relevant stakeholders, including employees, investors, and partners. Foster a culture of transparency and alignment, encouraging open dialogue and collaboration to achieve shared goals.

12.3 Financial Management and Budgeting

Effective financial management and budgeting are fundamental to the success and sustainability of any business. In this section, we will explore key principles and strategies for managing your business finances and creating a solid budget.

Financial Planning: Start by developing a comprehensive financial plan that outlines your business's financial goals and strategies. This plan should include a sales forecast, expense projections, and cash flow analysis. By setting clear financial objectives and creating a roadmap to achieve them, you can better allocate resources and make informed financial decisions.

Budgeting: A well-crafted budget serves as a financial roadmap, guiding your business's spending and ensuring that resources are allocated effectively. Start by identifying all revenue streams and categorizing expenses into different categories, such as operations, marketing, overhead, and personnel. Set realistic budget targets for each category, ensuring that your expenses align with your revenue projections.

Cash Flow Management: Cash flow is the lifeblood of your business. It is crucial to manage your cash inflows and outflows effectively to ensure smooth operations and financial stability. Monitor your cash flow regularly, maintain sufficient working capital, and be proactive in managing receivables and payables. Implement cash flow forecasting to anticipate potential shortfalls or surpluses and take necessary actions to maintain a healthy cash position.

Cost Control: Effective cost control is essential for maintaining profitability and maximizing financial resources. Regularly review your expenses and identify areas where you can reduce costs without compromising quality or efficiency. Consider negotiating better deals with suppliers, optimizing inventory management, and exploring cost-saving strategies, such as outsourcing or implementing technology solutions.

Financial Analysis: Conduct regular financial analysis to assess your business's performance and identify areas for improvement. Use financial ratios, such as profitability ratios, liquidity ratios, and efficiency ratios, to evaluate your business's financial health and compare it to industry benchmarks. Analyze trends, identify strengths and weaknesses, and make data-driven decisions to optimize your financial performance.

Debt Management: If your business has debt, it is crucial to manage it effectively. Develop a debt management strategy that includes regular debt servicing, minimizing interest costs, and considering refinancing options if feasible. Ensure that your debt obligations are manageable and align with your business's cash flow and revenue projections.

Investment and Growth Opportunities: Assess investment and growth opportunities carefully. Evaluate potential return on investment, risks involved, and alignment with your business goals. Whether it's expanding into new markets, investing in technology, or acquiring assets, make strategic investment decisions that will contribute to long-term growth and profitability.

Seek Professional Advice: Consider engaging the services of a financial advisor or accountant who specializes in small business finance. They can provide valuable insights, offer financial expertise, and help you navigate complex financial matters. Their expertise can assist in developing financial strategies, optimizing tax planning, and ensuring compliance with financial regulations.

12.4 Marketing and Branding Strategies

Marketing and branding are critical components of building a successful business and attracting customers. In this section, we will explore effective marketing and branding strategies to help you promote your products or services, reach your target audience, and build a strong brand presence.

Identify Your Target Market: Start by clearly defining your target market. Understand their demographics, preferences, needs, and purchasing behaviors. Conduct market research and gather customer insights to create buyer personas that represent your ideal customers. This understanding will guide your marketing efforts and help you tailor your messages to resonate with your target audience.

Develop a Unique Value Proposition: Your unique value proposition (UVP) is what sets your business apart from competitors. It highlights the unique benefits and value that your products or services offer to customers. Craft a compelling UVP that clearly communicates why customers should choose your business over others. Focus on the specific problems you solve, the benefits you provide, and what makes your offerings different.

Brand Identity: Establish a strong brand identity that reflects your business's values, personality, and positioning in the market. Develop a memorable brand name, logo, tagline, and visual elements that consistently represent your brand across all marketing materials and touchpoints. A strong brand identity builds recognition, trust, and loyalty among customers.

Marketing Channels: Identify the most effective marketing channels to reach your target audience. This could include digital marketing channels such as social media, search engine optimization (SEO), email marketing, content marketing, and paid advertising. Traditional marketing channels like print media, radio, television, and direct mail may also be relevant depending on your target market. Develop a comprehensive marketing plan that utilizes a mix of channels to maximize your reach and exposure.

Content Marketing: Create valuable and engaging content that educates, entertains, or solves problems for your target audience. Develop a content marketing strategy that includes blog posts, articles, videos, infographics, and other forms of content. Share your content on relevant platforms and establish yourself as a trusted authority in your industry. Content marketing helps drive traffic to your website, boost brand awareness, and generate leads.

Social Media Marketing: Leverage social media platforms to connect with your target audience, build brand awareness, and engage with customers. Identify the social media channels that your target audience frequents and develop a social media strategy to effectively reach and communicate with them. Regularly post engaging content, interact with followers, and use social media advertising to expand your reach and drive conversions.

Customer Relationship Management (CRM): Implement a CRM system to manage and nurture customer relationships. This system allows you to track customer interactions, capture valuable data, and personalize your marketing efforts. Use CRM to segment your customers, send targeted messages, and provide personalized experiences that enhance customer satisfaction and loyalty.

Monitor and Measure: Continuously monitor and measure the effectiveness of your marketing efforts. Utilize analytics tools to track key performance indicators (KPIs) such as website traffic, conversion rates, social media engagement, and return on investment (ROI). Regularly analyze the data to gain insights into customer behavior, identify successful marketing campaigns, and make data-driven decisions to optimize your marketing strategies.

Chapter 13: Financial Planning and Wealth Management

Section 1: Setting Financial Goals

Understanding the importance of setting financial goals
Identifying short-term, medium-term, and long-term financial goals
Prioritizing goals based on their significance and timeline
Developing a clear and actionable plan to achieve financial goals

Section 2: Budgeting and Expense Management

Creating a budget to track income and expenses
Differentiating between needs and wants
Implementing strategies to reduce expenses and save money
Monitoring and adjusting the budget as needed

Section 3: Saving and Investing

Importance of saving money for future financial security

Exploring various saving options such as savings accounts, certificates of deposit (CDs), and money market accounts
Introduction to different investment vehicles like stocks, bonds, mutual funds, and real estate
Assessing risk tolerance and diversifying investment portfolio

Section 4: Retirement Planning

Understanding the significance of retirement planning
Exploring retirement savings options like employer-sponsored retirement plans (e.g., 401(k), 403(b)) and Individual Retirement Accounts (IRAs)
Estimating retirement expenses and determining the required savings
Strategies for maximizing retirement savings and taking advantage of tax benefits

Section 1: Setting Financial Goals

Setting financial goals is the crucial first step towards achieving financial success. Without clear goals in mind, it becomes challenging to make strategic decisions and stay focused on a desired financial trajectory. In this section, we will explore the importance of setting financial goals and provide practical guidance on how to establish goals that align with your aspirations and values.

1.1 Understanding the Significance of Financial Goals
Financial goals serve as a roadmap for your financial journey. They provide direction, purpose, and motivation to make sound financial decisions. By setting goals, you give yourself a target to aim for, which helps you stay disciplined and committed to your financial plan.

1.2 Identifying Short-term, Medium-term, and Long-term Goals

To create a well-rounded financial plan, it is essential to identify goals that span different time horizons. Short-term goals typically involve achieving objectives within the next one to three years, such as building an emergency fund or saving for a vacation. Medium-term goals typically have a time frame of three to ten years, such as purchasing a home or funding higher education. Long-term goals extend beyond ten years and often revolve around retirement planning and wealth accumulation.

1.3 Prioritizing Goals Based on Significance and Timeline
Not all goals are equal in terms of importance or urgency. It is vital to prioritize your goals based on their significance and timeline. Evaluate which goals are most important to you and consider the potential impact they will have on your life. Rank them in order of priority, ensuring that you focus your efforts and resources on the goals that matter most.

1.4 Developing a Clear and Actionable Plan
Once you have identified and prioritized your financial goals, the next step is to develop a clear and actionable plan to achieve them. Break down each goal into smaller, manageable steps and establish a timeline for accomplishing each milestone. Consider the resources, skills, and knowledge required to reach your goals, and be prepared to adapt and adjust your plan as circumstances change.

1.5 Tracking Progress and Celebrating Milestones
Regularly monitoring your progress is essential to stay motivated and on track. Set up measurable benchmarks and track your achievements along the way. Celebrate reaching milestones, no matter how small, as they represent progress towards your larger goals. Recognize your accomplishments and use them as fuel to propel yourself forward.

1.6 Revisiting and Adjusting Goals as Needed
Life is dynamic, and circumstances may change over time. It is important to regularly revisit and evaluate your financial goals to

ensure they align with your evolving needs, aspirations, and financial situation. Adjust goals as necessary, taking into account any changes in income, expenses, family circumstances, or personal ambitions.

By setting clear and meaningful financial goals, you lay the foundation for a purposeful financial journey. This section provides you with the tools and insights to define your goals, prioritize them effectively, and develop a robust plan of action. Remember, your financial goals are unique to you, so take the time to reflect on what truly matters and build a path towards achieving your dreams.

Section 2: Budgeting and Expense Management

Effective budgeting and expense management are fundamental aspects of financial success. By creating a budget and monitoring your expenses, you gain control over your finances, make informed spending decisions, and allocate your resources wisely. In this section, we will delve into the importance of budgeting and provide practical guidance on how to create and manage a budget that supports your financial goals.

2.1 Creating a Budget
Creating a budget is the first step towards financial stability. A budget is a comprehensive plan that outlines your income, expenses, and savings goals. Start by gathering all relevant financial information, including your sources of income, bills, loans, and regular expenses. Categorize your expenses into essential (such as housing, utilities, and groceries) and discretionary (such as entertainment and dining out). Allocate a portion of your income to savings and emergency funds.

2.2 Tracking Income and Expenses
To effectively manage your finances, you need to track your income and expenses diligently. Use tools such as budgeting apps, spreadsheets, or financial software to record your income and expenses regularly. This helps you gain a clear understanding of

your cash flow, identify spending patterns, and make necessary adjustments.

2.3 Differentiating Needs and Wants

Distinguishing between needs and wants is crucial when allocating your financial resources. Needs are essential expenses required for your basic well-being, such as food, shelter, and healthcare. Wants, on the other hand, are non-essential expenses that provide enjoyment but are not necessary for your survival. Evaluate your spending habits and ensure that your needs are prioritized over wants to maintain financial stability.

2.4 Implementing Strategies to Reduce Expenses

Reducing expenses is a key component of effective budgeting. Explore strategies to minimize costs without compromising your quality of life. This may include negotiating bills, shopping around for the best deals, utilizing coupons or discount codes, buying in bulk, or seeking alternative, cost-effective options. Small adjustments in your spending habits can lead to significant savings over time.

2.5 Monitoring and Adjusting the Budget

A budget is not a static document; it requires regular monitoring and adjustment. Review your budget periodically, ideally on a monthly basis, to ensure that you are staying on track. Compare your actual income and expenses with the budgeted amounts and make adjustments as necessary. This flexibility allows you to adapt to changes in your financial situation or unexpected expenses.

2.6 Developing Financial Discipline and Mindful Spending

Developing financial discipline is essential for successful budgeting. Practice mindful spending by making conscious choices about where and how you allocate your money. Avoid impulsive purchases and take time to evaluate whether an expense aligns with your financial goals. Cultivate positive financial habits such as saving before spending and avoiding unnecessary debt.

2.7 Seeking Professional Guidance

If budgeting seems overwhelming or you need expert advice, consider seeking help from financial professionals, such as financial planners or budgeting coaches. They can provide personalized guidance, offer insights into effective money management strategies, and help you create a budget tailored to your specific needs and goals.

By implementing effective budgeting and expense management practices, you gain control over your finances and make intentional decisions that support your financial goals. This section equips you with the knowledge and tools necessary to create a realistic budget, differentiate between needs and wants, reduce expenses, and develop the financial discipline needed for long-term financial success. Remember, budgeting is an ongoing process that requires commitment and regular review to ensure your financial stability and prosperity.

Section 3: Building Wealth Through Investing

Investing is a powerful tool for building wealth and achieving financial goals. By intelligently allocating your money in different investment vehicles, you can potentially generate significant returns over time. In this section, we will explore the principles of investing, various investment options, and strategies to help you build wealth and secure your financial future.

3.1 Understanding the Power of Compound Interest
Compound interest is the key to long-term wealth accumulation. It refers to the interest earned on both the initial investment and the accumulated interest. By reinvesting your earnings, you allow your investments to grow exponentially over time. Start investing early to take full advantage of the power of compound interest and maximize your returns.

3.2 Setting Financial Goals
Before diving into the world of investing, it's crucial to establish clear financial goals. Define your short-term, medium-term, and long-term

objectives. Whether it's saving for a down payment on a house, funding your child's education, or building a retirement nest egg, having specific goals helps you make informed investment decisions aligned with your aspirations.

3.3 Assessing Risk Tolerance
Investing involves inherent risks, and understanding your risk tolerance is essential. Assess your willingness and ability to withstand fluctuations in the value of your investments. Consider factors such as your age, financial obligations, and long-term financial goals. This evaluation will guide you in selecting investment options that align with your risk appetite.

3.4 Diversification Strategies
Diversification is a fundamental principle of investing. Spreading your investments across different asset classes, industries, and geographical regions can help mitigate risk and enhance potential returns. Explore various investment options, including stocks, bonds, real estate, mutual funds, and exchange-traded funds (ETFs), to build a well-diversified portfolio.

3.5 Understanding Different Investment Vehicles
Investing offers a wide range of options, each with its unique characteristics and considerations. Familiarize yourself with stocks, bonds, mutual funds, ETFs, real estate, and other investment vehicles. Learn about their potential returns, risks, liquidity, and tax implications. This knowledge will empower you to make informed investment decisions.

3.6 Investing in Stocks
Stocks represent ownership in a company and can offer significant returns over time. Understand the basics of stock investing, including how to research and analyze stocks, evaluate company fundamentals, and assess market trends. Consider your investment horizon, risk tolerance, and diversification strategies when building a stock portfolio.

3.7 Investing in Bonds

Bonds are debt securities issued by governments, municipalities, and corporations. They provide a fixed income stream and are generally considered lower-risk investments than stocks. Learn about different types of bonds, such as government bonds, corporate bonds, and municipal bonds. Understand their risk-return profile and how they fit into your investment strategy.

3.8 Real Estate Investing

Real estate can be an excellent long-term investment, offering both income generation and potential appreciation. Explore different avenues of real estate investing, such as rental properties, real estate investment trusts (REITs), and real estate crowdfunding. Understand market dynamics, property valuation, and the financial aspects of property ownership.

3.9 Mutual Funds and ETFs

Mutual funds and ETFs offer diversification and professional management. Learn about their structure, fees, and investment strategies. Understand the difference between actively managed funds and passively managed index funds. Evaluate their historical performance, expense ratios, and alignment with your investment goals.

3.10 Risk Management and Asset Allocation

Proper risk management and asset allocation are critical to successful investing. Understand your risk tolerance and establish an appropriate asset allocation strategy that aligns with your goals. Consider factors such as your investment horizon, financial obligations, and target returns. Regularly review and rebalance your portfolio to maintain your desired asset allocation.

3.11 Staying Informed and Seeking Professional Advice

Investing is a dynamic field, and staying informed is essential. Continuously educate yourself on investment trends, economic factors, and market conditions. Follow reputable financial news sources, read investment books, and attend seminars or webinars.

Consider seeking guidance from financial advisors or investment professionals to help you navigate the investment landscape.

Section 4: Business Ideas and Entrepreneurship

Entrepreneurship offers a pathway to financial independence and the opportunity to turn your innovative ideas into successful ventures. In this section, we will explore various business ideas, entrepreneurial strategies, and key considerations for starting and managing your own business. Whether you aspire to launch a startup, become a small business owner, or pursue a side hustle, this section will provide valuable insights and practical advice.

4.1 Identifying Business Opportunities
The first step in entrepreneurship is identifying viable business opportunities. Look for gaps in the market, emerging trends, or untapped customer needs. Conduct market research, analyze industry dynamics, and assess the competitive landscape. Identify areas where your skills, expertise, or passion can be leveraged to create value and meet customer demands.

4.2 Creating a Business Plan
A well-crafted business plan serves as a roadmap for your entrepreneurial journey. Outline your business concept, target market, competitive analysis, marketing strategies, and financial projections. A business plan helps you clarify your vision, set achievable goals, and secure funding if necessary. It also acts as a reference document to track your progress and make adjustments along the way.

4.3 Financing Your Business
Securing adequate financing is crucial for launching and growing your business. Explore different funding options, including personal savings, bank loans, venture capital, angel investors, crowdfunding, and government grants. Evaluate the pros and cons of each option, considering factors such as interest rates, repayment terms, equity dilution, and eligibility criteria.

4.4 Building a Strong Team

A successful business is built on the foundation of a strong team. Surround yourself with talented individuals who share your vision and complement your skills. Hire employees or collaborate with freelancers or contractors based on your business needs. Develop effective communication channels, foster a positive work culture, and empower your team to contribute their best to the success of the business.

4.5 Marketing and Branding Strategies

Effective marketing and branding strategies are essential for business growth and customer acquisition. Develop a comprehensive marketing plan, including online and offline marketing channels, social media campaigns, content creation, and targeted advertising. Build a strong brand identity that resonates with your target audience, differentiates your business, and communicates your unique value proposition.

4.6 Sales and Customer Relationship Management

Successful businesses understand the importance of sales and customer relationship management. Develop sales strategies, establish sales targets, and train your sales team to effectively communicate the value of your products or services. Implement customer relationship management (CRM) systems to track customer interactions, gather feedback, and nurture long-term customer relationships.

4.7 Operations and Supply Chain Management

Efficient operations and supply chain management are crucial for business success. Develop streamlined processes, optimize inventory management, and ensure timely delivery of products or services. Explore outsourcing options, negotiate favorable vendor contracts, and implement quality control measures to maintain consistent product or service standards.

4.8 Financial Management and Budgeting

Sound financial management is essential for the long-term sustainability of your business. Develop a robust financial plan, including budgeting, cash flow management, and financial forecasting. Monitor key financial indicators, track expenses, and implement strategies to improve profitability. Consider consulting with accountants or financial advisors to ensure compliance and make informed financial decisions.

4.9 Scaling and Growth Strategies
As your business matures, scaling and growth become important objectives. Explore expansion opportunities, whether through opening new locations, diversifying product lines, or entering new markets. Develop strategic partnerships, explore joint ventures, or consider mergers and acquisitions as avenues for growth. Continuously evaluate your business strategy and adapt to changing market dynamics to stay ahead.

4.10 Embracing Innovation and Adaptability
In today's fast-paced business environment, embracing innovation and adaptability is crucial. Stay updated with industry trends, technological advancements, and changing consumer preferences. Foster a culture of innovation within your organization, encourage creative thinking, and adapt your business model to meet evolving customer needs.

This section provides valuable insights and practical advice for aspiring entrepreneurs. Remember, entrepreneurship requires perseverance, resilience, and a willingness to learn from both successes and failures. Stay committed to your vision, seek continuous improvement, and seize opportunities to turn your business ideas into reality.

References

- o
  - o "The Intelligent Investor" by Benjamin Graham
  - o "A Random Walk Down Wall Street" by Burton Malkiel
  - o "Common Stocks and Uncommon Profits" by Philip Fisher
  - o "The Little Book of Common Sense Investing" by John C. Bogle
  - o "Security Analysis" by Benjamin Graham and David Dodd
  - o "The Essays of Warren Buffett" by Warren Buffett and Lawrence A. Cunningham
  - o "Fooled by Randomness" by Nassim Nicholas Taleb
  - o "One Up On Wall Street" by Peter Lynch
  - o "The Four Pillars of Investing" by William Bernstein
  - o "Thinking, Fast and Slow" by Daniel Kahneman